Married LIFE:

Building a Divorce Proof Marriage

REGGIE ROYAL

WESTBOW
PRESS®
A DIVISION OF THOMAS NELSON
& ZONDERVAN

WestBow Press books may be ordered through booksellers or by contacting:

WestBow Press
A Division of Thomas Nelson & Zondervan
1663 Liberty Drive
Bloomington, IN 47403
www.westbowpress.com
1 (866) 928-1240

ISBN: 978-1-5127-4300-5 (sc)
ISBN: 978-1-5127-4301-2 (hc)
ISBN: 978-1-5127-4299-2 (e)

Library of Congress Control Number: 2016907953

Print information available on the last page.

WestBow Press rev. date: 7/28/2017

The Apostle Paul told Timothy that the key to effective, breakthrough ministry was having the preachers and the message aligned with the Cornerstone (Christ). Today, we have many different preachers with many different types of messages, but very few are in alignment. The best chance for you and your marriage is to yield your heart and mind to water flowing out of an aligned vessel.

The book you hold in your hand contains a Christ-aligned message from the hearts of a Christ-aligned couple. On these pages, Reggie and London offer you not only what they know, but more importantly who they are and how they live. They are the real deal. I've spent public and private time with them beyond the lights, camera and action of ministry. I have seen and can testify that they honor the Lord and each other in their marriage. Because of their alignment with Jesus in preaching and in practice, YOUR life and YOUR marriage are about to get richer. Don't only buy the book. Don't just read it. Absorb it. Digest it. Put it into practice. Get yourself and your marriage in alignment with the Cornerstone.

~Michael T. Smith
Founder of THE CHURCH Group Worldwide
Atlanta, GA

The bible says that marriage is honorable and Pastors Reggie and London Royal have been an example for many couples for years. *Married Life: Building a Divorce Proof Marriage* is a book that will give us insight on how they have made it while so many are walking away from their covenant. Trust me this book will help you divorce proof your marriage.

~Pastor John Hannah
Sr. Pastor New Life Covenant Church
Chicago, IL

Pastor Reggie is a proven leader in establishing strong and healthy marriages. *Married Life: Building a Divorce Proof Marriage* is a must read for anyone interested in building a solid, a happy and successful marriage.

~Pastors Paul & Fiona Arthurs
Wheaton Christian Center

Pastor Reggie has written an impactful blue print on 10 keys to lock out outside influences that will divorce proof your marriage. This insightful book will help you to identify and understand your covenant place in the marriage, how to effectively communicate and grow to meet the needs of your spouse that will cause your marriage to experience heaven on earth!

~Pastor Dewayne Freeman
Dewayne Freeman Ministries

DEDICATION

This book is dedicated to my parents, Billy & Yvonne Royal. Thank you for being my first and greatest model for God's intent for marriage.

ACKNOWLEDGEMENTS

"None of us got to where we are alone. Whether the assistance we received was obvious or subtle, acknowledging someone's help is a big part of understanding the importance of saying thank you." ~Harvey Mackay

I would like to extend a pure expression of appreciation and gratitude to my Pastors, Mike and DeeDee Freeman. You all have inspired London and I on so many levels and have truly been instrumental in making our Marriage EZ! Thank you for continuing to stretch us beyond our ability and leading us in fully walking out God's purpose for our lives.

A special thank you is extended to all of the precious couples whom London and I have had the privilege of building relationships with in and outside of ministry. You all have been a blessing to us in many ways:

- Paul & Fiona Arthurs
- Terrance & Keisha Campbell
- Dewayne & Lisa Freeman
- John & Anna Hannah
- Keith & Heidi Hershey
- William & Andria Hudson
- James & Deborah Logan
- Michael & Connie Smith
- James & Sharon Ward
- Bill & Veronica Winston

It takes teamwork to make any vision manifest. I would like to thank our world class team that has dedicated their time, energy, talents and servanthood to this wonderful project that we pray impacts lives around the world. Nothing we do on this God-given marriage platform would be possible without the behind the scenes dedication and support of these precious people:

- Kelli Ballard
- Samuel Brown
- Chris & Moneak Clarke
- Tanika Fitzgerald
- Bryan & Jessica Gray
- Clyde Hall III
- Kemica Jamison
- Brenda Palmer
- Leonard & Cathy Palmer
- Jason Royal
- Yvonne Royal
- Charles & Aneesa Sergeant
- Carlton & Cheretta Smith
- The greatest community of believers in the world – Lifeline Church – Chicago and Lifeline Church – Monterrey

And last but certainly not least, from the depths of my heart, I thank my dear London! I am blessed beyond measure because I get to do life with you and our boys, Justin and Jaden Royal.

FOREWORD

There are countless self-help books that focus on a wide range of subjects, but I believe that this book, *Married Life: Building a Divorce Proof Marriage*, is a great tool to assist you in this thing called "Marriage". As a couple, Reggie and I have declared 'War on Divorce' and by reading this book and applying its principles, you can join us in this declaration.

For married couples, this book is a tool that offers practical tips on creating the foundation to a great lasting relationship, maintaining your already amazing relationship, and how to revitalize a stale relationship. No matter what state your relationship is in, you will be glad that you took the time to read and apply the principles listed inside.

Maybe you aren't married, or don't have the desire to be married, but everyone desires relational success. *Married Life: Building a Divorce Proof Marriage* offers nuggets and insight for you to apply to any relationship you encounter throughout everyday life.

This book is an all-around great read and I'm not just saying this because the greatest husband in the world wrote it, lol!! We have been married for 20+ years and have experienced situations where applying these same principles has kept us in the game, even when it gets tough. If we would have known and followed these principles early on in our marriage, the road would have been a whole lot easier. I thank the Good Lord for allowing us to now be trained and possess the ability to share the knowledge that we have gained with you.

Take some time now (Yes, right now!) to sit down and read this book. Keep an open mind and challenge yourself to apply the principles. There are even questions listed at the end of each chapter to ask yourself (truthfully) and to help you reflect on what you have just read. As you read and apply what you've learned, you shall experience the best of God in your marriage and ultimately in your life.

Happy Reading.....

London C. Royal

CONTENTS

INTRODUCTION

In today's world, one year is a long time to be married. Most people enter marriage with no intention of staying together. They enter marriage with all of the windows open so that if anything happens, they have easy access to leave. They enter marriage with options. The marriage altar is the place and time where many people tell some of the biggest lies. Husbands and wives stand before one another, making promises and commitments that they have no intention on carrying out. Too many couples are in love on Monday and broken up by Friday. Divorce among Christians is just as prevalent as it is among non-believers. A Barna Group study revealed that among adults who have been married, one-third (33%) have experienced at least one divorce. Born-again Christians were indistinguishable from the national average on the matter of divorce: 33% have been married and divorced.[1]

> Didn't the LORD make you one with your wife? In body and spirit, you are his. And what does he want? Godly children from your union. So guard your heart; remain loyal to the wife of your youth. "For I hate divorce!" says the LORD, the God of Israel. "To divorce your wife is to overwhelm her with cruelty," says the LORD of Heaven's Armies. "So guard your heart; do not be unfaithful to your wife." (Malachi 2:15-16)

It is time to declare war on divorce, especially in the body of Christ. Previous generations lacked the spiritual and relational resources that are

---

[1] "New Marriage and Divorce Statistics Released." *Barna.* Barna Group, 31 Mar. 2008. Web. 2 June 2015.

available today; yet, they fully embraced their marriage vows and kept the covenant, often staying together for several decades. Unfortunately, long successful marriages are not the norm in today's society. Most people simply want to maintain their selfishness. They want to marry, but continue to operate as if they are single. This mentality is a disaster waiting to happen. The present generations have the tools necessary to build a divorce proof marriage, yet they make decisions that totally go against the Word of God. There is absolutely no reason to divorce, regardless of the mistakes you made or the ones your spouse made. Love covers everything! Does it cover cheating? Absolutely! Does it cover bringing a baby into the marriage? Absolutely! God's Word reminds us of this truth.

> *Most important of all, continue to show deep love for each other, for love covers a multitude of sins.* (1 Peter 4:8)

While it may require counseling and constant communication, with the proper revelation of God's love, everything that happens in a marriage can be reconciled. In order to build a divorce proof marriage and remain committed to the vows you took on your wedding day, you must remember God's original intent of marriage. Learn to love your spouse as Christ loves the church.

> *And further, submit to one another out of reverence for Christ. For wives, this means submit to your husbands as to the Lord. For a husband is the head of his wife as Christ is the head of the church. He is the Savior of his body, the church. As the church submits to Christ, so you wives should submit to your husbands in everything. For husbands, this means love your wives, just as Christ loved the church. He gave up his life for her to make her holy and clean, washed by the cleansing of God's word.* (Ephesians 5:21-26)

Married Life: Building a Divorce Proof Marriage equips you for a victorious marriage. When you took your vows before Christ, you committed yourself to work through any issues that arise in your marriage. You committed to staying together for richer or for poorer, through sickness and in health, until you are parted by death. The wedding day is full of love, happiness and joy. However, many couples spend little time, if any, planning what to do when challenges come. God hates divorce, and believers should hate what God hates.

God has placed a special grace on my life for marriage and family. It is my heart's desire for His children to have relational prosperity. London and I have been married for 20 years and by the grace of God we are enjoying life together. Our marriage does not simply thrive because we love God; it is our commitment to making our marriage work that allows us to experience that Zoe life. Many people have successful careers, but failed marriages. They spend so much time learning how to please their bosses that they do not take the time to learn how to get along with their spouse. Just as we plan for success in every other area of our lives, we must plan for success in marriage. There is no money-back guarantee of success in marriage simply because we know God and are filled with the Holy Spirit.

Marriage is work! You must decide today that, regardless of the challenges that you face, divorce is not an option. Decide to do the work! Use the tools in this book and work the Word daily in your life and in your marriage. London and I have declared war on divorce. We are not only called to equip His people to stay together, but also to enjoy every day of the journey. As you read the pages of these chapters, expect to be challenged to build a stronger connection with your spouse. You will assess your marriage and find yourself asking some of the following questions: What did I *really* mean when I said my vows? Am I meeting the needs of my spouse? Is forgiveness holding me from experiencing joy in marriage? *Married Life: Building a Divorce Proof Marriage* will inspire you to take your marriage from good to great.

If you currently have challenges in your marriage, decide right now that your marriage *will work*. There is nothing more important in a marriage than a determination that it shall last. Force yourself to overcome every temptation to quit. When commitment is small, the marriage is unstable. I encourage you and your spouse to read this book together. If you use the tools, you will see a change for the better. You will see God move in your marriage in a way that you have never experienced before. If you are single or dating with the intent of being married, this book will give you the tools to build a divorce proof marriage from the very beginning of your covenant. You will learn what it takes to have a successful marriage and have fun while doing so. At the end of every chapter, you will find space for you and your spouse to write a declaration for your marriage, applying each tool to make your marriage stronger. There is also a confession for your marriage. Use this book to improve every area of your marriage. You may have mastered some areas, while others still need work.

Please join London and I in the war against divorce. May you be equipped, inspired, changed and blessed as you take the married life journey!

PART ONE: MARRIED LIFE

THE COVENANT OF MARRIAGE – GOD'S ORIGINAL DESIGN AND INTENT

The honeymoon season is a delightful time. It's the time where the newness of a young love is celebrated. It's the time where husband and wife get to know one another and enjoy each other on levels they have never experienced before. For many, it's the most satisfying times of the relationship. Unfortunately, the bliss in many marriages dissipates years, sometimes months, after the marital ceremony. This was not God's original design for marriage.

Marriage is the first covenant that God established on earth. It is part of God's ordained plan to provide the earth with a reflection of His love through man and woman. Marriage was made to glorify God. He established marriage as a covenant with Him, but the world has perverted it into a simple contract. A covenant with God should not be broken; however, a contract can be void with mutual agreement. Godly marriage between a man and a woman is a permanent commitment. If you are not ready to rid yourself of pride, selfishness and impatience, *do not get married*. Marriage is not about *you*! Your marriage should reflect the relationship that Christ has with His bride, the church.

It pleases God when His children work at making their marriages better and sweeter as time passes. Adam and Eve had a marriage made in Heaven divinely orchestrated by a perfect God. In order to be successful in this area, you must understand God's original design and intent for your marriage. When you understand and fulfill your Godly responsibility as husbands and wives, your marriage will be successful according to the will of God.

Adam was created first, which sets a precedence of authority over woman. Eve was created to be Adam's equal counterpart and helper. Your design determines your purpose. God commanded Adam and Eve to be fruitful and multiply (Genesis 1:28). Man was made to deposit seed. The woman was made to receive and carry the seed. Adam's instinct was to protect, provide and love Eve as his undeserved gift from God. Eve completely fulfilled the role of being a helper to her husband. She was his "Chief Encouragement Officer," his trusted adviser and his lover. Most of all, Eve embraced her role of submission to her husband. They built a marriage to last and it was one, even with its flaws, to model after in today's world. You must decide that your marriage will prosper.

Meeting the Needs of Your Spouse

*As the Scriptures say, "A man leaves his father and mother
and is joined to his wife, and the two are united into one."*
(Ephesians 5:31)

Marriage blends two hearts and two spirits in a way that anything that affects one person also affects the spouse. Marriage requires that you care for your spouse, just as you care for yourself. You really do become *one* when you get married. You do not get married simply to have your own needs fulfilled. It can be something great or small, but it is crucial that you and your spouse communicate your needs to one another prior to getting married. This must continue throughout your union. As your needs change, you must make them known to your spouse. Husbands and wives can sometimes give room for pettiness. They don't strive to meet the needs of the other person when their needs are continuously not met. They enter the marriage with unjustified expectations because they haven't communicated their physical, financial, spiritual and emotional needs. Whatever your emotional needs may include, you naturally do those things for your spouse, hoping they return the favor. Let's take a look at the essential needs of each spouse in marriage.

What Every Woman Needs

1. Affection

Most women need affection. The problem is many men equate affection with sex. Affection is a non-sexual expression of care expressed in various ways, such as hugging, kissing, touching, smiling, winking, back rubs, feet rubs and even love notes. When women do these things for you, they are often looking for the same in return. Women feel alienated and extremely lonely when their emotional need for affection isn't fulfilled.

Willard F. Harley, Jr. states, "Affection is the environment of the marriage; sex is the special event."[2] Husbands, affection communicates that you care about your wife. This makes her feel important to you. You can't keep hiding behind your past and how you were raised. If you come from a family that did not show affection to one another, meeting your wife's need for affection may not come naturally to you. You must learn the behavior. Ask her what she needs from you, and then do it out of routine until it becomes natural to you. Every woman needs affection, even if she has not verbally communicated that to you.

2. INTIMATE CONVERSATION

Women need intimate conversation. It is a deeper level of detailed and personal communication. True intimate conversation is sensitive and directly connected to the heart; thus, you should only engage in this type of communication with your spouse. If you are having this type of communication with someone else, you easily open doors for the enemy to tamper with your marriage. Affairs happen when you have intimate conversation with the wrong person. Couples talk a lot during courtship and sometimes, communication decreases during marriage. Because you fulfilled this need during courtship, your spouse expects it during the marriage. It is sometimes uncomfortable to look into your wife's eyes and talk about matters of the heart. It could be fearful, but you have to deal with it and engage in intimate conversation on a consistent basis.

3. HONESTY & OPENNESS

A woman feels secure when she has accurate information about her husband. Most of the time, men are the ones hiding or holding back

---

[2] Harley, William. "How to Meet the Need for Affection Letter #2." *How to Meet the Need for Affection Letter #2.* Marriage Builders, Inc., n.d. Web. 15 June 2015.

information. Men, you must be open and honest about your thoughts, feelings, habits, likes, dislikes, daily activities and your history. She needs to know about your personal weaknesses and feelings. If something were to come up in your marriage, she has braced herself to deal with your weaknesses. When the man is not open and honest, it leads to frustration and you won't have trust in that marriage. Your wife will always feel like you are not telling her something. Women have a keen sense of discernment. Women are like God; when they ask you something, most times, they already know the answer. Save yourself the trouble of jumping through hoops and lies. She already knows! When you are not open and honest, you put your wife in a position to interrogate you. She feels like she has to ask you questions just to get you to tell her the truth. You may feel like you are under radar, but you should ask yourself: What's under the microscope that I am not revealing? Women are quick! When you are talking, they are already at the next sentence. They are calculating things in their heads. Not only should you answer all the questions, but you also have to avoid these lies of silence. Men, you need to gladly volunteer information. Just tell her so that she doesn't have to ask you.

We all need to be like Jesus. He told us (the church, His bride) where He was going and that He was coming back one day for us. If you really love her, then why shouldn't she know everything? When you are open and honest, it provides a clear roadmap for adjustments in your marriage. You need to understand the make-up of your wife. You, as the leader of your home, may be graced to deal with things that your wife may not be able to handle. Sometimes, there are things that you shouldn't bring home to your wife. You must discern when to discuss those unique situations.

4. Financial Support

Women have a genuine need to feel secure. Your wife needs to know that she is safe and that you can provide for her every need. Both men and women desire financial success. Even if you don't have any money right now, you marry with the hope that things will be better. God's original intent is for the woman to manage the household without having any external work responsibilities. This is a process, a faith project. Have the agreement up front that you both will work if that's what it takes to make ends meet.

"But don't begin until you count the cost. For who would begin construction of a building without first calculating the cost to see if there is enough money to finish it? Otherwise, you might complete only the foundation before running out of money, and then everyone would laugh at you. They would say, 'There's the person who started that building and couldn't afford to finish it!' (Luke 14:28-30)

Some women expect for their man to work and make a living, but they don't want to work. A couple needs to communicate about this before marriage and come to a mutual agreement. If left unaddressed, it could put a strain on the marriage, making the husband feel like less than a man. We cannot violate the wisdom of God when it comes to this. Wisdom violated is chaos created.

5. FAMILY COMMITMENT

Your wife does not want to feel as if she has to do everything on her own. Men, family commitment is not just feeding your children and clothing them. It means being responsible and sharing in the responsibility for their development as children and young adults. It is spending time with your family and actually participating in the activity. It is sharing the responsibilities of the entire household. You can be watching a movie with your family, but if you're still working on your laptop, you are physically there, but not present and interactive. Commitment to your family means teaching them values. When you are slacking in your commitment, it feels like neglect to your wife. She begins to feel like everything falls on her.

WHAT EVERY MAN NEEDS

Wives, you married your husband because he did a great job at meeting your emotional needs during your courtship. While it is your prayer and expectation that he will continue to meet those needs throughout your marriage, it is also your responsibility to ensure that your husband's needs are fulfilled. Men and women have very different needs. It is a natural tendency to love your spouse according to your own needs or love language. It is critical to recognize what your husband needs, and do all that you can to meet those needs. Outlined below are the most important needs of men in marriage.

1. Sexual Fulfillment

Men have a frequent need for sex. Sexual fulfillment at home helps prevent a wandering spouse. If he is getting his needs met at home, he has no need to look elsewhere. Sex should never be interrupted, except for a time of prayer and fasting when you mutually agree (1 Corinthians 7:5). A spouse should never withhold sex as punishment or offer it as a reward. Many women are guilty of this. It should not even cross your mind. Your primary obligation as husband and wife is to please one another. When you try to please yourself, you are acting in selfishness.

> *Now regarding the questions you asked in your letter. Yes, it is good to abstain from sexual relations. But because there is so much sexual immorality, each man should have his own wife, and each woman should have her own husband. The husband should fulfill his wife's sexual needs, and the wife should fulfill her husband's needs. The wife gives authority over her body to her husband, and the husband gives authority over his body to his wife. Do not deprive each other of sexual relations, unless you both agree to refrain from sexual intimacy for a limited time so you can give yourselves more completely to prayer. Afterward, you should come together again so that Satan won't be able to tempt you because of your lack of self-control. I say this as a concession, not as a command.* (1 Corinthians 7:1-6)

Men, you should never force your wife into something that she is not comfortable doing. Women, you should never withhold yourself from your husband. He needs enthusiastic participation in sex and desires for his wife to be the aggressor at times. He wants you to get his attention!

2. RECREATIONAL COMPANIONSHIP

Wives, you should be your husband's number one fan! Be there to support him in everything that he does. Sometimes, he just wants you to be near him. Most times, couples are close in courtship; it must continue in marriage. It strengthens the relationship between you and your spouse. The same sacrifices that you made in the dating season must also occur in marriage. Whatever you did to get your spouse, you must continue doing to keep them. Women, ask your husbands what recreational companionship is for him. It is not just sports. Make up in your mind that you are going to enjoy the activities that excite your husband. Find hobbies that you both enjoy and make a point to do them together often. The couple that plays together stays together!

3. AN ATTRACTIVE SPOUSE

Men are visual. Women are good at keeping themselves together during the courtship phase. They do their hair, put their makeup on and dress nice. Sometimes as soon as women say, "I do," those things go out the window. Ladies, you must dress becomingly to catch his eye. Wear what your husband likes. Whenever you go out of the house, you should look your best. Your husband expects you to look a certain way for him. Yes, your husbands should love you for who you are, but they also love you for how you look. When you look good, your husband feels good and sticks his chest out quite a bit! You are a reflection of your husband! You are an individual and while you aren't forced to do what your husband likes, you should work constantly to impress your man, not other women.

SIX WAYS TO BECOME AND STAY ATTRACTIVE TO YOUR SPOUSE

1. Weight Control – Decrease the intake of sugar, salt, fat and fried foods.
2. Makeup – Use it as an enhancer to your natural beauty.
3. Hair – Get a hairstyle that your husband likes! Remember that you should be working to impress your spouse.

4. Dress Nice – Wear the clothes that are attractive to your husband. Husbands, keep your wife looking good.
5. Diet and Exercise – Take care of your body and control what you feed it. Make good choices.
6. Personal Hygiene – Maintain cleanliness and grooming of your external body.

4. DOMESTIC SUPPORT

Domestic support means creating a peaceful atmosphere, free of conflict, worry and stress. Husbands need their homes to be in order. They want to come home and be able to be comfortable and relaxed. Your husband is fulfilled when he has your domestic support. This need gets more difficult to meet when children are part of the marriage. When both spouses work, it is crucial to communicate roles and responsibilities so that the home is well kept. First, find out what your spouse wants and needs within the home. Create a plan and execute accordingly.

5. ADMIRATION

Women, be proud of your husband. Every man needs to be regarded and respected. Respect is a condition of being esteemed or honored. It is an attitude of deference, admiration and its regard. Wives, you must regard your husbands. It is a great motivation and inspiration for your husbands to live up to your expectations. On the other hand, criticism will make him defensive. If you always tell him what he is doing wrong, and you don't build him up or admire him, he will become defensive and shut you off. Men need to know when they have done wrong. Sometimes a woman will pull back and not tell him, but men need to know and accept when they have missed the mark.

> So again I say, each man must love his wife as he loves himself,
> and the wife must respect her husband. (Ephesians 5:33)

"Forsaking all others" is part of the vows you took when you married. Hidden behind those words were the high expectations that both of you would succeed in meeting each other's emotional and physical needs. Continually meeting your spouse's needs nourishes the growth in your marriage. If you fail to do so, frustration grows. The key to a successful marriage is unselfishness – putting your spouse's needs above your own. Fully examining these needs is a great way to look deeper into your marriage to determine your spouse's individual needs. Whether your marriage is in trouble or not, when spouses fulfill each other's needs, the marriage becomes stronger.

APPLYING MARRIED LIFE –
MEETING THE NEEDS OF MY SPOUSE

How can I better meet the needs of my wife?

_____

_____

_____

_____

_____

_____

How can I better meet the needs of my husband?

_____

_____

_____

_____

_____

_____

Our Confession to Better Meet the Needs of One Another:

_____

_____

_____

_____

_____

_____

_____

_____

_____

_____

PART TWO: 10 KEYS TO BUILDING A DIVORCE PROOF MARRIAGE

1. Understand Your Role
2. Revisit Your Vows Often
3. Become a Student of Agape Love
4. Check Your Spirit
5. Continually Mature in Communication
6. Be Quick to Forgive
7. Protect the Marriage Bed
8. Keep It Exciting
9. Leave and Cleave
10. Respect Your Spouse

Key 1: Understand Your Role

Then the Lord God formed the man from the dust of the ground.
He breathed the breath of life into the man's nostrils, and the
man became a living person. Then the Lord God planted a
garden in Eden in the east, and there he placed the man he had
made. The Lord God placed the man in the Garden of Eden to
tend and watch over it. (Genesis 2:7-8, 15)

When God created man, He immediately gave him an assignment. Adam's assignment was to tend and watch over the garden. He also gave Adam specific instructions about how to live in the garden. *But the Lord God warned him, "You may freely eat the fruit of every tree in the garden – except the tree of the knowledge of good and evil. If you eat its fruit, you are sure to die."* (Genesis 2:16-17) When a man is truly connected to God, He will give him clear instructions that he must follow to successfully lead his household. God saw that it was not good for man to be alone, so He promised to make a suitable helper just right for him. But before God presented Adam with his wife, he gave Adam a job. He was the first zoologist! He named all of the animals that God made.

Then the Lord God said, "It is not good for the man to be alone. I will make a helper who is just right for him." So the Lord God caused the man to fall into a deep sleep. While the man slept, the Lord God took out one of the man's ribs and closed up the opening. Then the Lord God made a woman from the rib, and he brought her to the man. "At last!" the man exclaimed. "This one is bone from my bone, and flesh from my flesh! She will be called 'woman,' because she was taken from 'man.'" This explains why a man leaves his father and mother and is joined to his wife, and the two are united into one. (Genesis 2:18, 21-24)

The role of a man in the earth and in God's Kingdom is very significant. Man is the founder of the family. He binds the family together. He is called to act responsibly, sensibly and mature. Men were made to be leaders. The sad reality is that many men don't fulfill their purpose and role for which God designed them. The problem is not that women aren't submitting to their husbands. The real problem is a lack of male leadership in the home. Women have assumed the leadership role in the home because men have failed to step up to the plate. Many women have lost trust and respect for their husbands. Therefore, they are uncomfortable following their husbands because the last time they did, they experienced problematic circumstances. It is not God's proper order for women to lead. When things are out of God's order, you will not experience favorable outcomes. Truthfully, most women do not want to lead. They prefer that a man lead them. When the man is out of order, the home is out of order.

The reason why many marriages fail is that men and women don't walk in their marital roles according to God's original intent. *Getting wisdom is the wisest thing you can do! And whatever else you do, develop good judgment* (Proverbs 4:7). Wisdom is the principle thing and once you have it, you can thrive in your happy, divorce proof marriage. You need a clear understanding of how to relate to your spouse. You do not lose your identity by adhering to God's standard for marriage. Follow His plan with an attitude of entrusting yourself to Christ. God has designed a blueprint for spouses that, when followed, creates a whole, fulfilling marriage.

The Bible explicitly states the proper order for man and woman.

> *Be ye followers of me, even as I also am of Christ. Now I praise you, brethren, that ye remember me in all things, and keep the ordinances, as I delivered them to you. But I would have you know, that the head of every man is Christ; and the head of the woman is the man; and the head of Christ is God.* (1 Corinthians 11:1-3 KJV)

Headship is authentic when it is in alignment with God's purpose and design for His sons and daughters. Without God, a man is only masculine. True manhood happens when a man is connected to God. It is time for men to fully comprehend the purpose for which they were designed.

There are five essential roles that a man needs to fulfill as a man of God, husband and father.

The role of God's man is to be:
1. The Lover of His Wife
2. The Protector of the Family
3. The Provider of the Family
4. The Priest of the Family
5. The Prophet of the Family

THE LOVER OF HIS WIFE

> *For husbands, this means love your wives, just as Christ loved the church. He gave up his life for her to make her holy and clean, washed by the cleansing of God's word. He did this to present her to himself as a glorious church without a spot or wrinkle or any other blemish. Instead, she will be holy and without fault. In the same way, husbands you ought to love their wives as they love their own bodies. For a man who loves his wife actually shows love for himself. No one hates his own body but feeds and cares for it, just as Christ cares for the church. As the Scriptures say, "A man leaves his father and mother and is joined to his wife, and the two are united into one." This is a great mystery, but it is an illustration of the way Christ and the church are one. So again I say, each man must love his wife as he loves himself, and the wife must respect her husband. (Ephesians 5:25-29; 31-33)*

Notice that there isn't anything in the above passage that speaks about being *in* love. The love of Christ is unconditional, never changing, constant and consistent. Being in love infers that you can fall *out of love*. When you choose to embrace the principles of love and continuously show love through actions, the Holy Spirit will manifest the feelings of love that your heart and soul seek. If you have accepted Jesus Christ as your Lord and Savior, you are required to follow God's Word.

"So fear the LORD and serve him wholeheartedly. Put away forever the idols your ancestors worshiped when they lived beyond the Euphrates River and in Egypt. Serve the LORD alone. But if you refuse to serve the LORD, then choose today whom you will serve...But as for me and my family, we will serve the LORD." (Joshua 24:14-15)

The Bible is not a feeling book. It is a choice book. You must decide to allow God to reign and rule in every area of your life. Loving God requires serving God. God won't force you to love Him. You must *choose* to love Him. Love is a disciplined choice that you must make over and over again.

God calls the man, Christ. This demonstrates that Christ's likeness and manhood are synonymous. God calls the wife, the church, which Jesus loved at all costs. You must choose to love your wife when she is not easy to love. When she is inconsistent, you must be consistent, like Christ is to the church. A godly man will love his wife through her inconsistency. If you do not discipline your thoughts and emotions, what you choose to love can kill you emotionally, financially, physically and mentally. You must decide that your marriage will prosper, despite the challenging circumstances you will face.

In the same way, you husbands must give honor to your wives. Treat your wife with understanding as you live together. She may be weaker than you are, but she is your equal partner in God's gift of new life. Treat her as you should so your prayers will not be hindered. (1 Peter 3:7)

THE PROTECTOR OF THE FAMILY

When God created men, he placed a burning desire to protect in them. It dates back to the Garden of Eden when Adam was assigned to tend to the garden. God instructed Adam that he could freely eat the fruit from every tree in the garden, except for the tree of knowledge of good and evil. If Adam ate from that tree, he would surely die. God provided Adam with clear boundaries and just as many men do today, Adam crossed the line.

The woman was convinced. She saw that the tree was beautiful and its fruit looked delicious, and she wanted the wisdom it would give her. So she took some of the fruit and ate it. Then she gave some to her husband, who was with her, and he ate it, too. (Genesis 3:6)

Immediately following their disobedience, Adam and Eve gained an intimate knowledge of good and evil. Their eyes were opened, they realized they were naked, and they hid because of their shame. The moment a man is out of communion with God, he runs and hides. He may stop attending church, decrease his time in the Word of God, or become hard to find by those who hold him accountable for his actions. God held Adam responsible for failing to protect Eve from the enemy's deception. Men, your role is to lead and protect your family. You cannot do so effectively when you are out of the will of God.

As a godly husband, you are responsible for physically protecting your family from hurt, harm and danger. God made you with greater physical strength than your wife. It is your responsibility to use this strength in the proper manner – to ensure that your wife and children feel secure, even when you are not around. Christ loved the church to the utmost, laying down His life for all people. Because God calls men to love their wives as Christ loves the church, you are to exemplify Christ in the same manner. You must be willing to lay down your life for your family.

Natural protection comes through spending quality time with your wife and children. Just because you are at home does not mean that you are *present* in the home. Eat dinner together as a family. Watch movies together or have family meetings where everyone can share their thoughts and feelings. Shut everything off and give your family your undivided attention often. Let them know that they are important to you above all else. You must be a positive and present example to your children in order to protect them from making foolish mistakes that can negatively affect their lives. Your children are watching everything you do, so be sure that you set godly examples for them. They are watching how you treat your wife, your family, your friends and even people that you do not know. Men, you have great influence over the actions of your sons and daughters. Your actions may be personal, but they are never private. They affect generations to come.

> *The LORD is longsuffering, and of great mercy, forgiving iniquity and transgression, and by no means clearing the guilty, visiting the iniquity of the fathers upon the children unto the third and fourth generation.* (Numbers 14:18 KJV)

It is also crucial to support your wife's and your children's goals. Motivate them along their paths to success. You can protect them from quitting or making bad mistakes through continual encouragement and support of their dreams. If your wife wants to go back to school or start her own business, work together to make it happen. You may need to share some household responsibilities on the days when she can't. This is a form of protecting and loving her the way that God designed. If your children develop passions for hobbies, sports or other activities, help them get involved. Attend their games and spend one-on-one time helping them to become better. These actions display love and protection in its greatest form.

You must also protect your family emotionally by resisting the temptation to use your strength to dominate over your wife and children. Although women are very strong, they are also delicate. *In the same way, you husbands must give honor to your wives. Treat your wife with understanding as you live together. She may be weaker than you are, but she is your equal partner in God's gift of new life. Treat her as you should so your prayers will not be hindered* (1 Peter 3:7). If you leave your wife unprotected, she will become vulnerable to attack and abuse physically and emotionally. In the same manner, you must learn how to discipline your children firmly, but in love so that you guide their hearts and bodies. *Fathers, do not aggravate your children, or they will become discouraged* (Colossians 3:21). You must provide loving leadership that protects with confidence and love.

Spiritual protection means that you cover your family in prayer and that you protect them from being deceived by the enemy or false doctrine. In order to achieve this, you must be in close and continual communication with Jesus Christ. He will give you everything that you need and desire to protect your family.

THE PROVIDER OF THE FAMILY

The husband is responsible for ensuring that the family's physical needs are met. Men, you were created to be the visionary for your homes. It is your responsibility to have a financial vision for your household. The biblical teaching regarding this matter is well defined. Before God presented Eve to Adam, He gave him a responsibility: to tend to the garden and to name all of the animals that the Lord brought to him.

> *If anyone fails to provide for his relatives, and especially for those of his own family, he has disowned the faith [by failing to accompany it with fruits] and is worse than an unbeliever [who performs his obligation in these matters].* (1 Timothy 5:8 AMP)

> *And out of the ground the LORD God formed every beast of the field, and every fowl of the air; and brought them unto Adam to see what he would call them: and whatsoever Adam called every living creature, that was the name thereof. And Adam gave names to all cattle, and to the fowl of the air, and to every beast of the field; but for Adam there was not found an help meet for him.* (Genesis 2:19-20 KJV)

Adam didn't receive his wife until *after* he had a job! Eve was created to be Adam's helpmeet, his right-hand woman. She was fashioned from Adam's rib. She was part of him. She was his perfect, complete complement and partner. Though she was the co-manager of Eden, she leaned, depended on and trusted him for guidance. It is the same in the family today. Your wife and family must feel secure and know, without any doubt, that you will provide everything they need. Your trustworthiness provides your wife with an increased sense of security.

> *And the Lord replied, "A faithful, sensible servant is one to whom the master can give the responsibility of managing his other household servants and feeding them.* (Luke 12:42)

Men, you are responsible for making the best decisions for your family, which should be God-led. Your wife is there as your faithful consultant. A good man will discuss family matters with his wife. The man of the home is responsible for having the last say, although that final decision should take into consideration his wife's recommendations. Men, don't be smart enough to marry your intelligent wife, yet be too dumb to listen to her.

THE PRIEST OF THE FAMILY

God gave men the role of being the priest of the family. You were created to be the spiritual leader of the home. In biblical times, the high priest was the supreme leader of the Israelites. They went to God on behalf of the people and they went to the people on God's behalf. They were required to exemplify holiness and be sanctified in the eyes of The Lord.

> They must be set apart as holy to their God and must never bring shame on the name of God. They must be holy, for they are the ones who present the special gifts to the LORD, gifts of food for their God. (Leviticus 21:6)

Husbands, it is your responsibility to be the spiritual covering for your family. You are the pastor, priest, bishop or elder of your home. Just as the priests of the Old Testament, you too must keep your life holy and pure before the Lord. You cannot effectively commune with God on behalf of your family if you are living a sinful life without repentance. You must be set apart from the ways of this world. As the priest of your family, it is your duty to live a life of prayer and intercession. You must communicate with the Father so that you can be fully equipped to lead your family. He will give you the wisdom to lead and guide according to His will for your lives. Your prayer life must be consistent and the peace of God should rule your heart and mind.

The Word of God must govern your life. Knowing and obeying God's Word equips you to live a life pleasing to God. In order to know how to live a life pleasing to God, set apart from the world and continually live in His will, you must know and act on the Word. Studying the Word increases your knowledge of who Christ is and the conditions you must fulfill to reap the harvest promised in the Word. Strengthening your faith helps you become an effective leader. Faith is defined as complete trust in, and reliance on, the Word of God. Becoming one with God through His Word builds your faith, which results in a higher level of confidence in leading your family. Teach the Word to your family and protect them from false doctrine. The Bible is your blueprint for living! It will guide your family through life's affairs. The Word of God keeps your family from making decisions that could lead down the wrong road. Protect your family from making mistakes and teach them how to counsel with God for divine direction.

The man of the family should set a solid example of what it means for God to be your first priority. The priests of the Old Testament brought sacrificial offerings into the temple as a sign of worship to God. Christ must be first in your life, your heart, your time, your money and all of your sacrifices. His Word reminds us that, *You must worship no other gods, for the LORD, whose very name is Jealous, is a God who is jealous about his relationship with you* (Exodus 34:14). Successfully fulfilling your role as a husband and father requires you to be the priest or pastor of your home.

THE PROPHET OF THE FAMILY

The Merriam-Webster Dictionary defines a prophet as, *"one who delivers messages that are believed to have come from God, one who utters divinely inspired revelations, one gifted with more than ordinary spiritual and moral insight or a spiritual seer."*[3] A prophet is a representation of God to His people, one who hears from and speaks for God. As a husband, your role is to continually commune with God so that you can hear from Him for your family. You are an earthly representation of Christ for your family. It is your duty to proclaim the gospel of faith and to provide biblical instruction and training for your household. You are the spiritual leader of your home. Your wife and children will follow you as you follow Christ. You are the messenger from God to your family. A prophet communicates what he or she has heard from God to encourage, equip and edify His

---

[3] N/A." *Merriam-Webster.* Merriam-Webster, n.d. Web. 08 July 2015.

people. You are to do the same for your family. There should not be any other person that speaks life into your wife and children the way that you do. Encourage and push them toward their destiny according to the promises and revelations that God has given to you concerning them! Constantly decree and declare good things for their future, destiny and purpose.

Men, you have a responsibility to tap into the wisdom of God so that you can effectively hear Him. You do this by becoming a student of the Word and by asking God for His supernatural wisdom. He has promised to give His wisdom to anyone who asks.

> *If any of you lack wisdom, let him ask of God, that giveth to all men liberally, and upbraideth not; and it shall be given him. But let him ask in faith, nothing wavering. For he that wavereth is like a wave of the sea driven with the wind and tossed.* (James 1:5-6 KJV)

Wisdom not only increases your knowledge of God's Word, but it gives you the ability to make wise decisions in difficult circumstances. Whenever you need wisdom, pray and ask Jesus for direction. Expect that God hears you and will provide clear direction to lead you and your family. After you have heard from God, you must have faith (the courage to obey) to step out and apply what you heard. Wisdom produces strategy and God has a strategy to overcome every obstacle.

God gave four young men (Daniel, Hananiah, Mishael and Azariah) an unusual aptitude for understanding every aspect of literature and wisdom. Whenever the king consulted them in any matter requiring wisdom and balanced judgment, he found them ten times more capable than any of the magicians and enchanters in his entire kingdom (Daniel 1:17, 20). They consulted God in all things, which resulted in rich wisdom and understanding that could only come from above. You must continually tap into the wisdom of Christ on the behalf of your family. It is your role as the prophet of your home.

> *So be careful how you live. Don't live like fools, but like those who are wise. Make the most of every opportunity in these evil*

days. Don't act thoughtlessly, but understand what the Lord wants you to do. (Ephesians 5: 15-17)

Husbands, you are called to be the lover of your wife, the protector of your family, the provider, the priest, and the prophet of your family. God has anointed you to lead, encourage, equip and edify everyone under your roof so that they will grow in Christ and fulfill their God-ordained purpose. After Christ, your family is your first and most important ministry. Fulfill your role. Declare that your marriage will work and that your family will be successful. Don't you dare give up on God, your wife or your family. You were created to successfully walk in these roles.

THE ROLE OF GOD'S WOMAN

We have been in a season of learning but not applying, hearing but not doing, knowing better but not doing better. The days are evil and I believe we are experiencing such chaos due to the breakdown of the family structure. We need a move of God. Moves of God result in change, repentance and doing something different. There cannot be a move of God without change. A move of God only comes by revelation and it requires different actions. Revelation is a convincing or conviction by the Word of God at the level of your understanding that births faith. Faith is the courage to obey, apply and do that which you have heard. When there is strategic teaching of the Word, you receive it, apply it, and then you reap results of freedom in your life. You must do what you have been taught. These principles don't mean anything if you know them, but fail to apply them. The Word of God is true! The truth that you know and apply will make you free (John 8:32). It does not make sense for you to have plenty of spiritual gifts, but you don't know how to treat your spouse. Just as the man has roles, God ordained women to embrace specific roles in their lives as well. Let's take an in-depth look at the role of God's woman.

THE ROLE OF GOD'S WOMAN

1. To Know Who You Are
2. To Embrace Submission

3. To be the Keeper of the Home
4. To be an Encourager
5. To have a Quiet Spirit

> *So God created human beings in his own image. In the image of*
> *God he created them; male and female he created them. Then*
> *God blessed them and said, "Be fruitful and multiply. Fill the*
> *earth and govern it. Reign over the fish in the sea, the birds*
> *in the sky, and all the animals that scurry along the ground.*
> (Genesis 1:27-28)

In Genesis, the first wedding takes place. God brought Eve to Adam. When he awakened, he was well aware of Eve's relationship to him. If you have been in a deep sleep (close communion) with God, you will be well aware upon the first approach if she is the woman for you. Adam had time in the presence of God so that he could clearly recognize anything that was presented to him. God created man and woman with different functions, roles and purposes. Your purpose determines your design. Man was made to deposit, give and release seed. Woman was made to receive and carry seed. Being a woman, your husband's helpmeet, requires that you successfully walk out your purposed roles.

TO KNOW WHO YOU ARE

You must know who you are and like who you are. How can you expect God to send a man into your life and love you when you don't value and love yourself? When you don't know who you are, you settle for less than God's best and purpose for your life. Because of the fall (sin), women have a tremendous ability to settle and to allow more from men than they should. This happens because they don't know who they are. Don't compromise your anointing and gift from God by settling because you are not comfortable in your own skin. Wait on God's best! The man is not always the blame. Men can only do what you allow them to do. Women, you are made in the image and likeness of God, which means the character of God is part of our innermost being. You should not feel worthless, depressed, neither shameful nor embarrassed because of who you are. God's Holy Spirit is ready and willing to work within you – in your heart and your mind. You are fearfully and wonderfully made. You are God's masterpiece, and His plans for you are perfect.

> *You made all the delicate, inner parts of my body and knit me together in my mother's womb. Thank you for making me so wonderfully complex! Your workmanship is marvelous—how well I know it.* (Psalm 139:13-15)

> *For we are God's masterpiece. He has created us anew in Christ Jesus, so we can do the good things he planned for us long ago.* (Ephesians 2:10)

> *I know what I'm doing. I have it all planned out—plans to take care of you, not abandon you, plans to give you the future you hope for.* (Jeremiah 29:11 MSG)

God can take care of you better than any man. If that man does not know God, he will not know how to take care of you. God will give you true revelation of who you are to Him when you really get to know who He is to you. Women of God, you cannot fulfill purpose or any role unless you deepen your relationship with God. Some of you need to stop looking for a man and get into the presence of God. Let Him mold you, heal any hurt and prepare you for what and who He is going to present to you.

> *As Jesus and the disciples continued on their way to Jerusalem, they came to a certain village where a woman named Martha welcomed him into her home. Her sister, Mary, sat at the Lord's feet, listening to what he taught. But Martha was distracted by the big dinner she was preparing. She came to Jesus and said, "Lord, doesn't it seem unfair to you that my sister just sits here while I do all the work? Tell her to come and help me." But the Lord said to her, "My dear Martha, you are worried and upset over all these details! There is only one thing worth being concerned about. Mary has discovered it, and it will not be taken away from her." (Luke 10:38-42)*

God is calling out to you to spend time at His feet, for it is there where you will find yourself. In the verses above, Mary chose the better thing. She forsook busyness to sit at the feet of Jesus. Choose to be still and let God finish what He has begun in you. Hide yourself in the Word. When you are full of the Word, your spiritual discernment will keep you from making mistakes. When you neglect to spend time with God, you lack the ability to discern what is from Him and what a trick of the enemy is.

To Embrace Submission

God called the woman to be a helper, not a hindrance. Hurt women who have an incorrect revelation of true submission often pass it on to generations behind them. Submission is a principle of the Kingdom. It is an attitude of the heart. It is a decision to come under, to yield to the authority of another. In marriage, it is tough to submit to what you don't respect. However, biblically, you *must* submit. Lack of respect for your husband does not release you from submission. The Bible does not say to submit to your *good* husband or your *saved* husband. God simply commands that you submit to *your* husband. Women, you have been trying to turn your husbands' hearts by your own doing. Your prayers, submission to his leadership and the example of your life will turn his heart. The heart of the king is in the hand of the Lord and He turns it. You are not your husband's Holy Ghost! You must first submit to the Lord. Remember, you are not to violate the Lord's principles of submission.

> And further, submit to one another out of reverence for Christ. For wives, this means submit to your husbands as to the Lord. For a husband is the head of his wife as Christ is the head of the church. He is the Savior of his body, the church. As the church submits to Christ, so you wives should submit to your husbands in everything. For husbands, this means love your wives, just as Christ loved the church. He gave up his life for her to make her holy and clean, washed by the cleansing of God's word. He did this to present her to himself as a glorious church without a spot or wrinkle or any other blemish. Instead, she will be holy and without fault. (Ephesians 5:21-27)

Submit to Christ first and then to your husband. Submit to your husband before you submit to your pastor. You will never win your husband over by putting your spiritual leaders above him. You will cause him to resent you, your pastor and the body of Christ. If your husband mistreats you, God will deal with him accordingly.

> *In the same way, you husbands must give honor to your wives. Treat your wife with understanding as you live together. She may be weaker than you are, but she is your equal partner in God's gift of new life. Treat her as you should so your prayers will not be hindered* (1 Peter 3:7).

Women, when you need your husband to change or meet your needs, go to God. He will give you wisdom and a plan of action. Never get caught off guard operating in your flesh because you will always miss wisdom. *If you need wisdom, ask our generous God, and he will give it to you. He will not rebuke you for asking* (James 1:5). The flesh profits nothing! If you are in the flesh, you will always lose. Your husband is under the authority of God and He will deal with his heart. Stay submitted because submission activates Heaven.

To be the Keeper of the Home

Women were ordained to function as the homemaker. This is much more than cooking, cleaning, washing and managing other household tasks. Song of Solomon describes a homemaker as honorable, righteous, a supporter, and a developer, pure, disciplined, cultured, educated, elegant, civilized, of moral excellence and respectable. Women, you should carry yourselves as such even before you get married. When you are operating in those descriptors, you become set apart and desirable. Your home is your first ministry. It is a profession of its own. Blessed is the husband who has the livelihood that allows his wife to stay home. It is not God's original intent for a woman to work. Working women came with the fall of Adam and Eve. The day will come where men will take their rightful place in their homes and have the livelihood for their wives not to work. This can only happen by tapping into the scripture and working the

Word! Until then, women don't put undue financial pressure on your husband. Contribute financially by working until God provides a way for you to stay home.

> Even while we were with you, we gave you this command: "Those unwilling to work will not get to eat." (2 Thessalonians 3:10)

Ask God to give you grace to balance home, work and children. Proverbs 31 provides the biblical, balanced description of a homemaker:

> A truly good wife is the most precious treasure a man can find! Her husband depends on her, and she never lets him down. She is good to him every day of her life, and with her own hands she gladly makes clothes. She is like a sailing ship that brings food from across the sea. She gets up before daylight to prepare food for her family and for her servants. She knows how to buy land and how to plant a vineyard, and she always works hard. She knows when to buy or sell, and she stays busy until late at night. She spins her own cloth, and she helps the poor and the needy. Her family has warm clothing, and so she doesn't worry when it snows. She does her own sewing, and everything she wears is beautiful. Her husband is a well-known and respected leader in the city. She makes clothes to sell to the shop owners. She is strong and graceful, as well as cheerful about the future. Her words are sensible, and her advice is thoughtful. She takes good care of her family and is never lazy. Her children praise her, and with great pride her husband says, "There are many good women, but you are the best!" Charm can be deceiving, and beauty fades away, but a woman who honors the LORD deserves to be praised. Show her respect— praise her in public for what she has done. (Proverbs 31:10-31 CEV)

God intended for a woman to be balanced. She should be able to manage the responsibilities at home and out of the home, as well. Part of the role in homemaking is to, *Similarly, teach the older women to live in a way that honors God. They must not slander others or be heavy drinkers. Instead, they should teach others what is good* (Titus 2:3). God wants you to provide wisdom to the younger women to love their husbands and children, to live wisely and be pure. Teach them to work in their homes, to do good, and to be submissive to their husbands so that they do not bring shame upon the word of God (Titus 2:4-5). A woman that is successful in this role is successful in her marriage.

To be an Encourager

Some of you are where you are today because your mothers, grandmothers or other influential women in your lives encouraged, supported and developed you. It is the role of every woman to support and help develop others in their gifts, callings and graces, including her husband. Some men just need a good word from a good woman. Don't belittle or discourage him. Encourage him to become who God destined him to be. It is your role to be a spiritual help and encouragement to your husband. Protect him and never expose his areas of weakness to others.

Never beat your husband down with your words. God pulled the woman from the rib, which protects the heart. It is your job to protect your husband's heart. Cover him just as he covers you. *A wise woman builds her home, but a foolish woman tears it down with her own hands* (Proverbs 14:1). Even in your frustration, build up your husband. He should feel confident that he is able to become all that God destined him to be. When the world tells him that he can't, reiterate to him that he can. When he feels like a loser at work, make him feel like a winner at home. You should be the sole person that he can always come to for words of affirmation, inspiration and reassurance. You should be his Chief Encouragement Officer!

To Have a Quiet Spirit

Every man wants a woman with a quiet spirit. It is unattractive when a woman has a loud spirit. One of the quickest ways to get a man to run away from you is to be a Chatty Cathy or a nagger. How do you know if you are a nagger? You never stop or rest on an issue. You are usually the innocent partner or you ask certain questions with evident answers to get your point across. Let everything you say be good and helpful so that your words will be an encouragement to those that hear them.

> *Let your conversation be gracious and attractive so that you will have the right response for everyone.* (Colossians 4:6)

> *It's better to live alone in the corner of an attic than with a quarrelsome wife in a lovely home.* (Proverbs 25:24)

A contentious woman is controversial, debatable and talkative. A quiet spirit does not require a quiet woman. A strong, godly man doesn't want a woman that will allow him to run over her.

> *Don't use foul or abusive language. Let everything you say be good and helpful, so that your words will be an encouragement to those who hear them.* (Ephesians 4:29)

Some of you have great men, but you don't realize it. It stems from ungodly training, lack of preparation for marriage, and negative interaction with your spouse. You have pushed him into a corner with your words, so he has become defensive. You can do more to change him through prayer, than you can do with your words. The Lord is responsible for turning the heart of your husband, not you. When you keep nagging and harassing with your words, you push him further away and you make him doubt how he feels about you. You cannot keep doing the same things and expect different results. Take that same aggressiveness and bombard Heaven with your prayers. Real men want and need a woman with a quiet spirit. If you have a quiet spirit, you can hear God clearly! Take your needs to God. He will deal with you, and then He will change your husband's heart and mind to give you what you need.

Hear the Word, do the Word and you will get Word results.

APPLYING MARRIED LIFE – UNDERSTANDING YOUR ROLE

How can I better fulfill my role as a husband?

_____

_____

_____

_____

_____

How can I better fulfill my role as a wife?

_____

_____

_____

_____

_____

Scriptures to Stand on to Fulfill Roles in Marriage:

_____

_____

Our Confession to Walk in our Roles as Husband and Wife:

_____

_____

_____

_____

_____

_____

_____

_____

KEY 2: REVISIT YOUR VOWS OFTEN

Most couples truly love one another and want to make their marriages work, but they simply don't know how. They talk to people who don't rely on biblical standards for marriage and they embrace other doctrines that are not founded on the Word of God. It is time to declare war on divorce, especially in the body of Christ. Previous generations lacked the spiritual and relationship resources that are available today, yet they fully embraced their marriage vows and kept the covenant by staying together for decades.

> *Didn't the L*ORD *make you one with your wife? In body and spirit you are his. And what does he want? Godly children from your union. So guard your heart; remain loyal to the wife of your youth. "For I hate divorce!" says the L*ORD*, the God of Israel. "To divorce your wife is to overwhelm her with cruelty," says the L*ORD *of Heaven's Armies. "So guard your heart; do not be unfaithful to your wife.* (Malachi 2:15-16)

There needs to be a breakdown of the vows before marriage so that couples have a full understanding of the promise before they commit. Many people enter marriage with no intention of staying in it forever. The wedding day has passed, the honeymoon is over, and now reality has set in. You return home and after a few years, sometimes even months, you realize that marriage is serious business. It is two people coming together with both of their historic creations and generational mindsets. Some people are ready to run when the noise of life comes, but you both must be sure that the noise doesn't get loud enough for you to not hear or remember the vows that you made at the altar before God.

Many times, couples look at the wedding pictures and the wedding videos, and reminisce about the beautiful day. Rarely, do couples ponder their vows. They often become vague memories tucked away with the wedding dress, invitations and other keepsakes. Forgetting or neglecting the promises you made to your spouse can hinder the growth of your marriage. Your vows should serve as hallmarks – reminders of who you are, why you are married, and what God is calling you to do together. When you took those vows, you not only made a promise to your spouse, but also to God. It is better not to make a vow than to make one and not keep it.

> When you make a promise to God, don't delay in following through, for God takes no pleasure in fools. Keep all the promises you make to him. It is better to say nothing than to make a promise and not keep it. (Ecclesiastes 5:4-5)

Here is an example of the vows that you may have made at the altar:

> In the presence of God, I take you to be my lawfully wedded wife/husband. To have and to hold from this day forward. For better or for worse. For richer, for poorer, in sickness and in health. I promise to love you unconditionally, to support you in your goals, to honor and respect you, to laugh with you and cry with you. I take you with all your faults and your strengths as I offer myself to you with my faults and strengths. I will help you when you need help, and I will turn to you when I need help. I choose you as the person with whom I will spend my life from this day forward until death do us part.

Focus on these: *For better or for worse. For richer or for poorer. In sickness and in health.* Keep these close to your heart so when those things happen, you're not quick to run out. Challenges are a reality of what happens in life. It means with money or without money. When you are sick and when you are well. Nothing gives you the right to go outside of your marriage. You made a vow to love your spouse unconditionally, and it is your responsibility and command by God to honor them! Marriage is serious business. You can do more together than apart. *A person standing alone can be attacked and defeated, but two can stand back-to-back and conquer. Three are even better, for a triple-braided cord is not easily broken* (Ecclesiastes 4:12).

Too many marriages lack respect. Husbands and wives battle for respect, and this should not be the case. If you love your spouse, you will respect them. You will support them in their goals. You must choose your spouse over and over again until you two are parted by death. Resolve in your heart that your marriage is forever. Once you acknowledge that you will spend the rest of your life with this person, all of your decisions will be based on the foundation that you set in your heart – that your marriage will last. Your vows should act as a compass for your marriage. When using them as such, you and your spouse will have the ability to change course when you are headed in the wrong direction.

Suggestions for Revisiting Your Vows Often

1. Review and recite your vows with your spouse on a regular basis. Look into one another's eyes and renew the promises within your heart.
2. Keep your vows visible in your home.
3. Renew your vows with one another on your wedding anniversary.
4. Break down the vows and discuss how you all have or have not kept them in your marriage. Create a plan to do better in the areas that need work.

APPLYING MARRIED LIFE –
REVISITING YOUR VOWS OFTEN

How can I ensure that I keep my vows to my wife?

_____

_____

_____

_____

_____

How can I ensure that I keep my vows to my husband?

_____

_____

_____

_____

_____

Scriptures to Stand on to Keep Our Vows:

_____

_____

Our Confession to Revisit Our Vows Often:

_____

_____

_____

_____

_____

_____

_____

_____

KEY 3: BECOME A STUDENT OF AGAPE LOVE

Agape is the Greek word for love. It means affection, esteem, good will and benevolence[4]. Agape love is the ultimate kind of love. It is self-sacrificing and equivalent to the love Christ displayed for His own children on the cross. God calls us to love others just as He has loved us. This God kind of love is the same love that you should have for your spouse. Paul said in Ephesians 5:1-2 that we are to, *Imitate God, therefore, in everything you do, because you are his dear children. Live a life filled with love, following the example of Christ. He loved us and offered himself as a sacrifice for us, a pleasing aroma to God.* Jesus' great love for us, even as sinners, led Him to sacrifice His life so that we may live. Love is what is most important to Christ. Jesus said, *"So now I am giving you a new commandment: Love each other. Just as I have loved you, you should love each other. Your love for one another will prove to the world that you are my disciples"* (John 13:34-35).

Marriage is a journey of sacrifice and selflessness. Your love for your spouse should be equivalent to the kind of love that Jesus displays for us daily. When people look at how you treat your spouse and how you love him or her, they should see the love of God at work in your marriage. Loving with a sacrificial love requires continual learning and renewing of your mind. Love is more than those warm, fuzzy feelings. It is an attitude that reveals itself through actions. True love in marriage is directed outward, toward your spouse rather than inward toward yourself. This kind of love is not what the flesh yearns to do. It requires

---

[4] Strong's Greek Lexicon Search Results." *Strong's Greek Lexicon Search Results.* N.p., n.d. Web. 08 Mar. 2016.

God's supernatural power to flow in your mind and heart, which will equip you to love your spouse with the love of Christ.

> *Love is patient and kind. Love is not jealous or boastful or proud or rude. It does not demand its own way. It is not irritable, and it keeps no record of being wronged. It does not rejoice about injustice but rejoices whenever the truth wins out. Love never gives up, never loses faith, is always hopeful, and endures through every circumstance.* (1 Corinthians 13:4-7)

First Corinthians 13:4-7 displays the love that you should exhibit towards your spouse. God calls you to be patient with their shortcomings, mistakes and downfalls. You should not be jealous of your spouse or be in competition with one another. Don't allow your insecurities and insufficiencies to prevent you from loving your spouse with agape love. The two of you should be one another's biggest supporter and encourager. If the wife gets a raise, the husband gets one, too. You are building a life together and everything you have should be fully merged together, including your financial accounts. Having separation and independence in marriage displays that you love your spouse, but you don't trust them.

Marriage is about meeting your spouse's needs, not always getting your needs met. You cannot demand your own way and expect to have a joyful marriage. Marriage is sowing and reaping. If you struggle with this, ask God to help you set aside your own desires to meet the needs and wants of your spouse. Agape love does not expect anything in return. Love does not fly off the handle, nor is it irritable. Love keeps no records of wrongdoing. This means that once you forgive your spouse for something, you should not silently keep track of them hurting or disappointing you. Your spouse is not perfect and neither are you. You must give them grace. Forgiveness is a requirement of walking in love. Love never gives up! You may need to counsel with a professional to repair issues in your marriage, but you must endure through every circumstance with your spouse. God demands you to do so and He hates divorce.

David Nelmes defines agape love as unconditional love that is always giving. It's impossible to be a taker when you have agape love. It devotes total commitment to seek your highest best, no matter how anyone may respond. This form of love is totally selfless and does not change, whether the love is returned or not. This is the original and only true form of love.[5] Agape love is unconditional, wholehearted, unqualified, unreserved and unlimited. You are required to give this love to your spouse, regardless of how they treat you or respond to the love you give. Love covers everything! *Most important of all, continue to show deep love for each other, for love covers a multitude of sins* (1 Peter 4:8).

Loving your spouse with sacrificial (agape) love is only possible when Christ is in your heart and His Holy Spirit lives in you. Think about how Christ loves you, even when you neglect to spend time with Him, neglect to obey His Word, or fail to walk in your calling. He never stops loving you! He still wakes you up every morning, protects you and provides for you. Christ is always standing with His hands open wide to receive you with pure love in His heart. That is the kind of love marriages should display. So many marriages are failing today because husbands and wives don't have God as the primary focus of the marriage. God designed marriage to mirror the covenant relationship that He has with His children. Becoming a student of agape love requires that you study the Word and the character of Jesus. It also requires that you increase your prayer life. Admit to Him that you cannot exhibit agape love without His help. Spend time in His presence so that you can learn how to release His power to love when you are impatient, unkind, unforgiving or irritable. Ask God to renew the joy of your salvation and to eliminate any pride from your heart that may be keeping you from loving your spouse with agape love.

You cannot love like Christ if you don't have full revelation of how He loves others. Christ healed sinners, ate with them and fed them. His love was not dependent upon if they loved Him the same. He saw all people as equal and loved them absent of their beliefs and circumstances. If Jesus can do this for strangers, surely you can do this for your spouse – the one that you chose as your partner for the rest of your life.

---

[5] God Is Agape Love." *God Is Agape Love.* Exilon, 10 Nov. 2007. Web. 08 Mar. 2015.

APPLYING MARRIED LIFE –
BECOME A STUDENT OF AGAPE LOVE

How can I better display agape love to my wife?

_____
_____
_____
_____
_____

How can I better display agape love to my husband?

_____
_____
_____
_____
_____

Scriptures to Stand on Regarding Agape Love in Our Marriage:

_____
_____

Our Confession to Continually Display Agape Love to One Another:

_____
_____
_____
_____
_____
_____
_____
_____
_____

KEY 4: CHECK YOUR SPIRIT

How do you treat your spouse when no one is looking? Do you deal with them in love, truth and compassion? Do you talk down to them, disrespect them or refuse to submit to one another? Do you take out your frustrations, disappointments or past experiences by dealing with your spouse in a perfidious manner? Marriage is an institution of God. It is the covenant on earth that allows you to triumph over any challenging situation you encounter. Marriage is where you should feel safest with your past experiences, your present emotions and your future goals and dreams. It should be a relationship full of joy, honor, esteem, respect, integrity and celebration. It's full of obligations, rewards, growth and manifested promises of God. Marriage is the mirrored image of Christ's love for us. You should always treat your spouse as such. It is an unending union between Christ and His bride – the Church. Marriage is the most intimate connection that ties two human beings together. Every part of your life is intertwined with your spouse. Marriage makes you one flesh.

The disappointment lies in what marriages have been reduced to in today's society. The enemy has done his best work to pervert God's original intent for marriage. Divorce has become so prevalent because people don't want to submit to God or to one another. The laws of God are being broken every time we turn our heads. Within our marriages, we deal treacherously with one another and it results in the dissolution of too many marital covenants. Divorce has become a convenient option and not often regarded for what it is – a sin.

Have we not all one father? hath not one God created us? why do
we deal treacherously every man against his brother, by profaning

the covenant of our fathers? Judah hath dealt treacherously, and an abomination is committed in Israel and in Jerusalem; for Judah hath profaned the holiness of the LORD which he loved, and hath married the daughter of a strange god. The LORD will cut off the man that doeth this, the master and the scholar, out of the tabernacles of Jacob, and him that offereth an offering unto the LORD of hosts. And this have ye done again, covering the altar of the LORD with tears, with weeping, and with crying out, insomuch that he regardeth not the offering any more, or receiveth it with good will at your hand. Yet ye say, Wherefore? Because the LORD hath been witness between thee and the wife of thy youth, against whom thou hast dealt treacherously: yet is she thy companion, and the wife of thy covenant. And did not he make one? Yet had he the residue of the spirit. And wherefore one? That he might seek a godly seed. Therefore take heed to your spirit, and let none deal treacherously against the wife of his youth. (Malachi 2:10-15 KJV)*

In the text above, we see that Judah committed an abomination by dealing treacherously with his brother, with God and with his spouse. It tells the story of men getting rid of their Hebrew wives to get remarried to pagan women. God exposes and condemns their treachery, especially within their marriages. Dealing treacherously means to break covenant; to separate an agreement; to forsake a formal loyalty; to disconnect. When you sin against your marriage and the vows that you made to your spouse, you sin against what is pure and holy to God. He set marriage apart for a very special purpose and meaning in the life of His people. Marriage is God's idea; thus, we are not allowed to define it or change it to tickle our fleshly desires. We must conform to what God has established. When you deal with your spouse in a treacherous manner, it often comes from what has hit your spirit, either prior to your marriage or what you all have gone through in your marriage.

Guard your heart above all else, for it determines the course of your life. (Proverbs 4:23)

If the course of your life comes out of your heart, you have to keep a clean one. Don't allow anyone else to contaminate your heart, and you must keep from contaminating it, as well. Anything that gets into your spirit will come out in your living, whether positive or negative. You have a great responsibility to guard your heart and check your spirit. If you aren't constantly taking heed to your spirit, you will allow all types of seeds to be sown into your spirit. The way you think and act is a reflection of your previous environment and life experiences. Experiences that you have gone through years ago may have taken root in your spirit. When issues of your past become evident to others, it is clear that it has been inside of you for a long time and has now worked its way out. It has manifested in the way that you deal with others. This is why it is so crucial that you, *let God transform you into a new person by changing the way you think. Then you will learn to know God's will for you, which is good and pleasing and perfect* (Romans 12:2). Changing how you think can change the course of your life. But many of us continue to live treacherously and it spills onto how we treat others, especially our spouses.

> *An offended friend is harder to win back than a fortified city. Arguments separate friends like a gate locked with bars.*
> (Proverbs 18:19)

Offense that hits your heart and spirit will cause you to break covenant with your spouse. Offense will always cause you to deal treacherously with your spouse. Holding on to what your spouse has done to offend you will not harm them. It does more harm to you. It doesn't cut off God *to you*; it cuts you off from God. You can pray fervently, but your situation won't change until you release the person that offended you. The small cracks prevent your marriage from flourishing. Offense is a heart issue, and you must filter what you allow to come in and set up root in your heart. Managing your heart is continuous work, and you must manage it appropriately. Because all of your life flows out of your heart, you should give great attention to what you allow to hit your heart. The Word will wash and cleanse everything that is in your heart.

And then shall many be offended, and shall betray one another,
and shall hate one another. And many false prophets shall rise,
and shall deceive many. (Matthew 24:10-11 KJV)

Offense is the breeding ground for deception. It causes you to isolate yourself, even if it only exists in your thinking. It allows someone or something other than the Word of God to minister to your spirit. Offense is like worry; it is subtle. It has a strong tendency to whisper the wrong things to you. No one wakes up and says, "I think I'll leave my spouse today." The root of offense starts small, but builds over time. Offense looks for agreement. So if your spouse offended you, be very careful with whom you choose to share your situation. Even the right person can speak the wrong thing, which can take you back to the place where you deal with your spouse treacherously. The offense that hits your spirit will cause you to break covenant. Offense means to make angry, to arouse resentment, to insult, to assault or attack, to cause displeasure or to cause to stumble. Many times, offense happens because of how you perceived what your spouse did or said to you. Offense is bait that leads to a trap. Offense is a spirit that will not let you go. It is your responsibility to release the offense from your heart and spirit. People make some of the most brutal decisions out of offense!

TRUTHS ABOUT OFFENSE

1. Offense is subtle and will cause you to doubt things of which you used to be sure. (John 1:29-34, Matthew 11:2-3)
2. Offense usually occurs when something hits too close to home. Your spouse may not have said something nasty or mean to you. It probably just happened to hit a sensitive spot in your life. Sometimes you may be offended by your spouse because there is something you haven't dealt with that is still lingering in your spirit. In reality, your spouse hasn't done anything wrong to you. (1 John 3:11-12)
3. Offense occurs when your unjustified expectations remain unmet. (2 Kings 5:1-13)

KEY 4: CHECK YOUR SPIRIT

4. Offense can cause you to miss breakthrough. It is the enemy's job to pull you away from your marriage so that you miss what God has for you. (Matthew 18:7)

5. Your ability to handle offense is an indication of your spiritual maturity.

What you say to your spouse and the manner in which you say it can cause your spouse to be offended. Your words have the power to hurt and kill. Stop running over your spouse with your mouth! Offense is designed to isolate you from one another. It enables the enemy to get you away from God's plan and purpose for your marriage. That is what happens when you build walls around your heart due to the offense, which you refuse to release. You think that you are hurting your spouse because they offended you, but you are hurting yourself when you continue to hold on to the offense. A spirit of offense will never let you go. You have to let it go. Holding on to offense is a choice, and so is letting go. You don't have a right to be offended and not release your spouse from the offense. The spouse who chooses to hold to an offense, as opposed to releasing and forgiving, has either forgotten or never understood what they did and the times they needed forgiveness. Your spouse has not done more to you than what you have done to Jesus. Don't allow offense to stay in your spirit. It hinders the prosperity of your marriage.

Offense that has hit your spirit causes you to go into protection mode. Whatever hits your spirit literally causes you to become like the Dead Sea in Israel. Unlike the Sea of Galilee, which receives water from the north and gives water to the south, the Dead Sea receives water into it, but nothing goes out of it. So everything in it dies. When you are offended, nothing can flow through you. Everything backs up. Everything that used to flow well in your marriage has the tendency to die. When you are in protection mode, you become a primary candidate for betrayal. You seek your own protection or benefit at the expense of your spouse. You don't quit your job when your boss offends you. So why would you allow offense to hinder your marriage from thriving? *Work willingly at whatever you do, as though you were working for the Lord rather than for people* (Colossians 3:23), especially in your marriage. If you don't deal with betrayal, you will end up in hatred. The enemy hates unity, agreement and anything that is in line with the plan of God for your life. He wants to keep you and your spouse fighting, bickering, complaining and fussing. He wants to keep you offended. When you refuse to check your spirit, guard your heart and release offense, you please the enemy and disappoint God.

Offense very seldom works both ways. We want to control how people see us. We want our spouses to look at our actions, words and know our hearts, but we don't extend the same grace to them. We judge our spouses by what they say or do, but want them to look at our hearts rather than our actions. However, you won't break an agreement if you take heed to your spirit, which requires that you guard and protect your heart. As long as you live, you will be hurt, offended, abused and used, especially by those that are closest to you. Take heed to your spirit--the real you--your inner man, so that you will not hinder the success of your marriage. When you do this, the love between you and your spouse will continue to blossom.

APPLYING MARRIED LIFE – CHECK YOUR SPIRIT

What, if anything, has hit my spirit that has remained unchecked? How does it affect my relationship with my wife?

_____

_____

_____

_____

_____

What, if anything, has hit my spirit that has remained unchecked? How does it affect my relationship with my husband?

_____

_____

_____

_____

_____

Scriptures to Stand on to Guard Our Hearts & Check Our Spirits:

_____

_____

Our Confession to Continually Check Our Spirits and Avoid Offense:

_____

_____

_____

_____

_____

_____

_____

Key 5: Continually Mature in Communication

Effective communication is a key ingredient for a successful marriage. The sad reality is that many spouses do not talk to one another. They spend ample time talking to friends, family, co-workers and even people they don't know, but they refuse to pour that same time and effort into talking to their spouse. Communication with your spouse is more than casual conversation. It is an intimate exchange that must occur to strengthen your union and continually meet the needs of your spouse. It involves listening, understanding and honesty. Communication is a process by which individuals or groups exchange information, utilizing a common system of symbols, signs or behavior. Communication comes in various forms. It is not only what you say to your spouse verbally that speaks to their heart. Your non-verbal actions and responses can speak much louder than the words that leave your mouth.

UCLA professor Albert Mehrabian developed one of the most well-known rules when it comes to communication. He determined that people receive messages best in non-verbal form. Albert's rule states that fifty-five percent of messages received and processed by the brain are based on body language. Thirty-eight percent of messages are processed based on tone of voice. Only seven percent of received messages are based off of words that are spoken verbally.[6] Non-verbal elements such as gestures, facial expressions and body language play an even greater role in determining how we interpret what is said.

---

[6] Non-Verbal Communication." *Arkadin Collaboration Services*. Arkadin, n.d. Web. 08 June 2015.

Communication can be complicated between spouses because men are logical thinkers and women are emotional feelers. Men speak what they think while women speak what they feel. Good communication involves speaking, listening and understanding. To communicate effectively is to transmit information, thoughts or feelings so that the other person can receive and understand it. The key to communication is understanding, and the key to understanding is listening. You must consider what is in the heart of your spouse when discerning what he or she says to you.

> *Wherefore my beloved brethren, let every man be swift to hear, slow to speak, slow to wrath: For the wrath of man worketh not the righteousness of God.* (James 1:19-20 KJV)

> *Understand [this], my beloved brethren. Let every man be quick to hear [a ready listener], slow to speak, slow to take offense and to get angry. For man's anger does not promote the righteousness God [wishes and requires.]* (James 1:19-20 AMP)

> *Wisdom is the principal thing; therefore get wisdom: and with all thy getting get understanding.* (Proverbs 4:7 KJV)

> *For the word of God is alive and powerful. It is sharper than the sharpest two-edged sword, cutting between soul and spirit, between joint and marrow. It exposes our innermost thoughts and desires.* (Hebrews 4:12)

Everything that you say or do sends a message to your spouse. Marriage does not demand perfection, but does require priority. Marriage is a learning environment in which both partners can grow and develop over time. Just as you plan for success in other areas of your life, you must do the same in your marriage. This includes continually developing effective communication with your spouse. What you communicate comes from your heart. *Death and life are in the power of the tongue: and they that love it shall eat the fruit thereof* (Proverbs 18:21 KJV). Life is speaking what God tells you to say to your spouse. Death is when you speak out of your flesh – your hurt, anger and pain.

> *Let nothing be done through strife or vainglory; but in lowliness of mind let each esteem other better than themselves.* (Philippians 2:3 KJV)

> *Brood of vipers! How can you, being evil, speak good things? For out of the abundance of the heart the mouth speaks.* (Matthew 12:34 NKJV)

You are responsible for what you verbally place in the heart of your spouse. Continually pour positive energy and encouragement into the mind and heart of your husband or wife. Speak life into him or her! Speaking life involves the following:

- Affirming your mate's character and actions
- Accepting your mate's strengths and weaknesses
- Encouraging your mate's destiny and potential
- Listening before you speak
- Repenting quickly
- Sharing the truth in love
- Forgiving even before your mate repents

Your spouse must be able to trust you with the deepest parts of his or her heart. Communication is what prevents and solves issues in marriage. It is impossible to have any kind of healthy relationship without communication. This is true for human relationships and relationship with God. Genuine communication should be open, honest and non-confrontational. It is important that couples are able to vent without attacking each other.

TEN KEYS TO EFFECTIVELY COMMUNICATING WITH YOUR SPOUSE:

1. **Uncover and expose what you feel and what you need**. Men are not mind readers, ladies. You have to tell your husband what you

need and expect from him. If you don't communicate what you need, you will be disappointed with your spouse. Your spouse cannot meet your needs if he or she is not aware of them.

2. **Be honest, but not hurtful.** Spend a lot of time talking to your spouse and deal in truth. When you deal in truth, be honest, but not hurtful. You cannot cut your spouse off at the knees and expect to have peace. Flowers, lingerie and candy cannot fix some things. So be careful of what you say to your spouse and how you say it. Too many people have sex despite issues. Sex is good, but it doesn't fix issues. When you are finished, the issues are still there, waiting on you all to solve them. Husbands, be totally open and honest with your wives.

3. **Hearing is not the same as understanding.** True communication happens when you speak to one another *and* confirm that what you heard *and* understood your spouse to say is really what he or she meant. Just because couples talk does not mean they understand one another. What your spouse says may not be what you hear. What you hear may not be what your spouse meant.

4. **Timing is important.** There is an ideal time to have every conversation with your spouse. You must correctly determine when the time is right. Use wisdom. If things become heated, operate within a three-day rule. Stop the conversation and return to it in a time that you all specify as right for the both of you.

5. **Stay away from aggressive conversation.** Don't use your conversation or words to punish your spouse. Be considerate. There is never a valid reason for anyone to yell. It is a clear sign of disrespect. Do not verbally abuse or degrade your spouse. You can even abuse your spouse without saying a word. The old saying goes, "If looks could kill, your spouse would be dead." Even your non-verbal responses can be hurtful. Non-verbal reactions can be worse than words. Take responsibility for the words you've sowed into your spouse that causes them to act a

certain way. Your negative responses can cause your spouse to shut down completely.

6. **Don't be reluctant to share the little things**. The little things turn into big things. The accumulation of small things can cause you to give up on your marriage because you grow tired. You love your spouse, but you feel like you cannot take anymore. Love can heal and restore everything if you pull away from your selfishness. There will be things about your spouse that you would love for them to change, but they never will. Pray for God to change your spouse. You have to resolve in your heart that if your spouse never changes, you will still love, respect and accept him or her the same. The first thing God will change is *you*. He will give you grace to deal with your spouse. Change your confession. Confession brings about what you want to see in your husband or wife. Confess it until you see it come to pass.

> *Catch all the foxes, those little foxes, before they ruin the vineyard of love, for the grapevines are blossoming!*
> (Song of Solomon 2:15)

7. **Communicate about an issue until it is resolved.** Many couples circle the same block, discussing the same issues, because the issues remain unsettled. Unless you and your spouse solve and bury the issues, they will appear again, most times with greater momentum. Get to the root of the issue. Settle and detach it so that it does not return. It does not matter how many times you need to talk about the issue. Don't walk away from it until it is settled. Clear and effective communication requires your undivided attention. It displays your honor and respect for your spouse, which is your first ministry.

8. **Adopt a win-win approach not a winner approach.** If you enter into a conversation with the goal of winning, you have already lost. If you walk away thinking, "I got her" or "I got him," you have both lost. You both must have a win-win attitude, which

means that you both have agreement, understanding, clarity and action steps to move forward, continually improving your communication. Stay focused on what is best for the marriage rather than your individual pleasures.

9. **Listen to your spouse's needs with a heart of understanding.** Clearly understand your spouse's intentions. You know your spouse better than anyone else. Based on what you know about your spouse, trust his or her heart.

10. **Don't make decisions without talking with your spouse.** You all are united in covenant. You must remain in agreement on all aspects of your life and relationship. If a major decision needs to be made that affects your household in any way, make the decision with your spouse. Refrain from discussing your marital business with other people, including your parents and best friends. Your marriage only involves you and your spouse.

Communication is to love what blood is to life. Couples must communicate effectively to have a successful marriage.

APPLYING MARRIED LIFE –
CONTINUALLY MATURE IN COMMUNICATION

How can I mature in communication with my wife?

_____

How can I mature in communication with my husband?

_____

Scriptures to Stand on to Improve Our Communication:

_____
_____

Our Confession to Continually Mature in Communication:

_____
_____
_____
_____
_____
_____
_____
_____
_____
_____
_____
_____
_____
_____
_____
_____
_____
_____
_____
_____

KEY 6: BE QUICK TO FORGIVE

And "don't sin by letting anger control you." Don't let the sun go down while you are still angry, for anger gives a foothold to the devil. (Ephesians 4:26-27)

Challenges in marriage are inevitable. Trials strengthen your marriage. You both are human, which means there will be times when you hurt one another's feelings or do something that angers the other. Because of the great love you have in your heart for your spouse, more than likely you won't intentionally hurt your spouse. However, it's bound to happen. When it does, both partners must be quick to apologize and quick to forgive. *Be gentle with one another, sensitive. Forgive one another as quickly and thoroughly as God in Christ forgave you* (Ephesians 4:32 MSG).

The Greek word for forgiveness is *aphesis*, which means to release. To forgive is to release. Stop holding grudges against your spouse and stop keeping record of their wrongs. God paid the ultimate price! His shed blood provided forgiveness for all people. Since He paid the price for you, He expects you to sincerely forgive others in your heart. When you refuse to do so, bitterness stands in the way of your prayers. *For if you forgive others their trespasses, your heavenly Father will also forgive you, but if you do not forgive others their trespasses, neither will your Father forgive your trespasses* (Matthew 6:14-15). A key ingredient for a divorce proof marriage is the ability to forgive quickly, repeatedly. You should not still be mad with your spouse two weeks after something has occurred. Talk about your issues, forgive, and move on. Stop manipulating them through your silence. Be quick and sincere in your apologies and don't allow disappointments to fester. The longer they fester, the longer your marriage will travel in the same circle as you attempt to move beyond a particular issue.

You will not be able to shake the inner torment that you experience if you refuse to forgive your spouse. How many times should you forgive them? Jesus said, "Seventy times seven," which means that you should forgive as often as your spouse needs. *Shouldn't you have mercy on your fellow servant, just as I had mercy on you?' Then the angry king sent the man to prison to be tortured until he had paid his entire debt. "That's what my heavenly Father will do to you if you refuse to forgive your brothers and sisters from your heart"* (Matthew 18:33-35). When you obtain the full revelation of how God forgives everything that you have done and will do, you will realize that you do not have the right to withhold forgiveness from your spouse.

When your spouse hurts you deeply, forgiveness may seem difficult. However, it frees you from bitterness and resentment toward your spouse. The power of darkness desires to destroy all godly marriages. Your willingness to forgive your spouse loosens Satan's grip on the issues within your relationship. Forgiving can be painful, but you must forgive and move on. Stop bringing up past issues because it causes your spouse to live through the offense again. Forgiveness is not lip service; it is love in action. It is refusing to inflict the penalty for the offense. Once forgiveness truly takes place, healing begins.

> *Go ahead and be angry. You do well to be angry—but don't use your anger as fuel for revenge. And don't stay angry. Don't go to bed angry. Don't give the Devil that kind of foothold in your life.* (Ephesians 4:26-27 MSG)

Here are some essential truths about forgiveness. Embracing these truths will open your heart to forgive your spouse, or anyone else, for any disappointment or hurt against you.

TEN FORGIVENESS TRUTHS

1. Forgiveness is the characteristic of the strong. The weak can never forgive.
2. Forgiveness is not for the faint-hearted.

3. Forgiveness is the mark of a true man and a true woman of God.
4. When you forgive, it's like setting a prisoner free: *you.*
5. Forgiveness does not change the past, but it does enlarge the future.
6. Unforgiveness delays spiritual victories, hinders worship, blocks prayers and disables the flow of healing in your life.
7. Healing begins with forgiveness.
8. Refusing to truly forgive a person demonstrates resentment, bitterness, and anger, none of which represents a true Christian.
9. Pride is at the root of unforgiveness.
10. Forgiveness is a decision, not an emotion.

You are required to forgive because Jesus Christ extended the same forgiveness to you. Unforgiveness is equivalent to the sin or hurt that your spouse imposed upon you! You, too, will need forgiveness from God and your mate, so how can you deny forgiveness? If you can't forgive, don't ask to be forgiven.

> *And why worry about a speck in your friend's eye when you have a log in your own? How can you think of saying to your friend, 'Let me help you get rid of that speck in your eye,' when you can't see past the log in your own eye? Hypocrite! First get rid of the log in your own eye; then you will see well enough to deal with the speck in your friend's eye.* (Matthew 7:3-5)

Don't allow your flesh to operate in unforgiveness. Even if your spouse does not repent, you must forgive. Make the decision to forgive even if you have not yet surrendered your anger, sadness or frustration to Christ. It will restore and rejuvenate your marriage. *Love prospers when a fault is forgiven, but dwelling on it separates close friends* (Proverbs 17:9).

> *O Lord, you are so good, so ready to forgive, so full of unfailing love for all who ask for your help.* (Psalm 86:5)

Applying Married Life – Be Quick to Forgive

How can I better walk in forgiveness as a husband?

_____

_____

_____

_____

_____

How can I better walk in forgiveness as a wife?

_____

_____

_____

_____

_____

Scriptures to Stand on to Quickly Forgive One Another:

_____

_____

Our Confession to Quickly Forgive One Another:

_____

_____

_____

_____

_____

_____

_____

_____

_____

KEY 7: PROTECT THE MARRIAGE BED

God created sexual intimacy for men and women to enjoy within the confines of marriage. The world has totally perverted this intimacy, which God created only for marriage. The enemy comes to steal, kill and destroy. He is after your marriage, and he will tempt you in areas where he knows that you or your spouse is weak. God commands that you walk by the Spirit and not gratify the lusts of the flesh. *So I say, let the Holy Spirit guide your lives. Then you won't be doing what your sinful nature craves. The sinful nature wants to do evil, which is just the opposite of what the Spirit wants. And the Spirit gives us desires that are the opposite of what the sinful nature desires. These two forces are constantly fighting each other, so you are not free to carry out your good intentions* (Galatians 5:16-17). To keep the marriage bed undefiled, you must remain vigilant and pure in thought, action and deed.

> *Give honor to marriage, and remain faithful to one another in marriage. God will surely judge people who are immoral and those who commit adultery.* (Hebrews 13:4)

> *Honor marriage, and guard the sacredness of sexual intimacy between wife and husband. God draws a firm line against casual and illicit sex.* (Hebrews 13:4 MSG)

> *Let marriage be held in honor (esteemed worthy, precious, of great price, and especially dear) in all things. And thus let the marriage bed be undefiled (kept undishonored); for God will judge and punish the unchaste [all guilty of sexual vice] and adulterous.* (Hebrews 13:4 AMP)

This scripture doesn't license you to do whatever you choose with your spouse. You both must agree about the boundaries that you set sexually within your marriage. God commands that you give honor (high respect or esteem) to your marriage. Sex is the most intimate interaction that you and your spouse experience. There is a sacredness of having sex with your spouse. You must protect the marriage bed! It is not just a physical place. You must keep your heart, your thoughts and your emotions pure in the sight of Christ and your spouse. If you are successful in this, your marriage bed will also remain pure.

> *But because there is so much sexual immorality, each man should have his own wife, and each woman should have her own husband. The husband should fulfill his wife's sexual needs, and the wife should fulfill her husband's needs. The wife gives authority over her body to her husband, and the husband gives authority over his body to his wife.* (1 Corinthians 7:2-4)

The marriage bed does not become impure overnight. Impurity first starts in the mind and then reflects itself in the physical realm. Husbands and wives, resist all temptations, major or minor, in order to protect the heart of your spouse and to keep your bed pure. *So humble yourselves before God. Resist the devil, and he will flee from you. Come close to God, and God will come close to you* (James 4:7-8). Sex or intimate fellowship (secret conversation, emails, texting, etc.) with someone other than your spouse is sin. This includes lust, impure thoughts and imaginations. If, and when you are tempted, you must be equipped to endure.

> *No temptation has overtaken you that is not common to man. God is faithful, and he will not let you be tempted beyond your ability, but with the temptation he will also provide the way of escape, that you may be able to endure it.* (1 Corinthians 10:13)

Submit yourself to God, resist the promptings of the enemy and he will flee from you. All intimacy, sexual and emotional, is reserved only for your spouse. If, and when, impure thoughts arise, you must, *destroy every proud obstacle that keeps people from knowing God. We capture their rebellious thoughts and teach them to obey Christ* (2 Corinthians 10:5). Communicate these impure thoughts to your spouse. Keeping secrets is dangerous.

Setting boundaries in your marriage assists you in keeping the marriage bed undefiled. Avoid intimate fellowship with those of the opposite sex, besides your spouse. You or your spouse should not have friends of the opposite sex that aren't mutual friends. You should never exchange emails, phone calls or text messages with the opposite sex without your spouse being aware of it. Solely focusing on your spouse heightens your level of sexual intimacy. Carve out time for fun and intimacy. Enjoy the caress of your spouse and give yourself to only him or her, willingly and joyfully. God designed sex for the two of you to enjoy. It is pure and beautiful in His sight.

APPLYING MARRIED LIFE – PROTECT THE MARRIAGE BED

What actions do I need to take as a husband to protect our marriage bed?

_____

_____

_____

_____

_____

What actions do I need to take as a wife to protect our marriage bed?

_____

_____

_____

_____

_____

Scriptures to Stand on to Protect Our Marriage Bed:

_____

_____

Our Confession to Protect Our Marriage Bed:

_____

_____

_____

_____

_____

_____

_____

_____

KEY 8: KEEP IT EXCITING!

The honeymoon phase of marriage is often the time where recreational companionship is viewed as an essential ingredient to the marriage. Newlyweds spend ample time engaging in leisure activities, taking vacations and exploring new experiences. This helps build a stronger emotional and physical bond between a husband and wife. Oftentimes, after being married for a little while, spouses get comfortable and stop doing the things that made them fall in love with one another. Couples simply exist; they don't grow. They move from being love mates to roommates, from roommates to cellmates, with the children as the wardens. Don't allow this to happen in your marriage! If you don't keep your marriage fresh and exciting, you will become bored.

Never become content or comfortable with your spouse. Keeping your spouse happy requires that you do more to keep them than you did to get them. Life commitments have the tendency to chip away at your time and eventually, the fun in your marriage. Many times couples run at the speed of light, and later realize that somewhere along the line they stopped enjoying each other. Routine has the potential to drive your marriage into a rut. You cannot allow this to happen. You must constantly pursue one another.

Men, it is your responsibility to keep chasing your wife and to make sure that she is worthy of being pursued. Spend some money on her. Get her hair done and get her some good makeup. She is tired of Maybelline and Fashion Fair just isn't fair anymore. Woman is the glory of man (1 Corinthians 11:7). It is your role to keep her looking the way you prefer. She can't remain worthy of your pursuit when you refuse to keep her looking beautiful. Ensure that she has all that she needs! Brothers, you have to look a certain way, as well. She wants you to be attractive to her! Iron your clothes, get clothes that fit, keep your underwear clean, and get manicures and pedicures. Get your hair cut and keep your mustache and beard trimmed. Be well groomed for your lady at all times. If you keep yourself attractive, your spouse will make changes and become more attractive to you.

Spouses must keep one another a top priority, even over family members, friends and the children. You cannot build your marriage around your children. They are going to grow up and leave the house, and it will be just you and your spouse again. You must put continual effort into enjoying one another in every season of your marriage. Ensure that you all find time to spend together, without the children. Never put your children before your spouse. It is imperative that you create balance between caring for and giving attention to your spouse while still showing love and attention to your children. *If you are a wife, you must put your husband first. Even if he opposes our message, you will win him over by what you do. No one else will have to say anything to him, because he will see how you honor God and live a pure life* (1 Peter 3:1-2).

Date your spouse in every season of your marriage. Boredom gives room to the enemy and causes your spouse to seek fulfillment in other places. Find new ways to speak to them according to their love language. In order for your spouse to meet your needs, you must communicate your desires. Wives, tell your husbands what excites you and what makes him more attractive to you. Husbands, you must do the same. Don't be afraid to tell your wife what makes her more attractive to you. Desires change as you grow, but you should always have your needs met. After you learn what your spouse needs, do all you can to fulfill their needs.

IDEAS TO KEEP YOUR MARRIAGE EXCITING

1. Schedule a weekend getaway for just you and your spouse (without the children).
2. Never stop dating each other. Have weekly date nights and choose a different activity or place each week. Find an activity that you both enjoy and do it weekly or monthly (golf, bowling, movies, bike riding, etc.)

3. Engage in health and wellness together (i.e., working out together, meal planning, etc.)

4. Pray together daily. You will develop spiritual intimacy in your marriage.

5. Cook meals together and engage in intimate conversation while doing so.

6. Have a little time apart from one another from time to time. It is important that husbands and wives spend time with their friends. (Disclaimer: This does not include friends of the opposite sex.)

7. Make sex fun and exciting (spontaneity, trying new things as long as your spouse agrees, set a romantic atmosphere in the home).

8. Leave love notes for your spouse.

Applying Married Life – Keep it Exciting

How can I commit to keep my marriage exciting for my wife?

_____

_____

_____

_____

_____

How can I commit to keep my marriage exciting for my husband?

_____

_____

_____

_____

_____

Scriptures to Stand on to Keep Our Marriage Exciting:

_____

_____

Our Confession to Attack Boredom and Keep Our Marriage Exciting:

_____

_____

_____

_____

_____

_____

_____

_____

_____

KEY 9: LEAVE AND CLEAVE (FORSAKING ALL OTHERS)

So the LORD God caused the man to fall into a deep sleep. While the man slept, the Lord God took out one of the man's ribs and closed up the opening. Then the LORD God made a woman from the rib, and he brought her to the man. "At last!" the man exclaimed. "This one is bone from my bone, and flesh from my flesh! She will be called 'woman,' because she was taken from 'man.'" This explains why a man leaves his father and mother and is joined to his wife, and the two are united into one. (Genesis 2:21-24)

Getting married is a life-altering event. You take on various roles throughout marriage. You become husband and wife, parents, partners in life, partners in business, and partners in ministry. It is vital that you continually remain focused on the ultimate purpose of marriage and the biblical requirements of this divine covenant with Christ. God made Eve especially for Adam and ordained that they be joined together in holy matrimony. As noted in the scripture above, God called them to unite into one flesh. In marriage, God's perfect will is for both the husband and wife to leave their parents and to cleave to one another.

Leaving your parents does not mean that you no longer honor them, spend time with them or respect them. It means that the new family you formed through marriage becomes your first priority. In Genesis 2:24, the Hebrew meaning of leave is "to forsake dependence upon, to release, leave behind and let go." Cleaving to your spouse means that you are committed to adhere firmly, closely, loyally and unwaveringly to one another.

In Matthew 19:6, Jesus said, *"Since they are no longer two but one, let no one split apart what God has joined together."* Unfortunately, leaving and cleaving never happens in many marriages. The danger is that it causes spouses to betray and lose respect for one another. When you share your marital challenges with others or rely on your parents to provide for your household, you essentially uncover your spouse. Leaving your parents in the biblical sense also means that you should not rely on them to help provide financially or make decisions for your household. Doing so will cause your spouse to feel insignificant and disrespected. Spouses that experience great difficulty leaving their parents create a lack of unity and intimacy within the marriage. Your unwavering commitment to your spouse helps you build a strong, divorce proof marriage.

Once you leave the altar, God is first priority and your spouse is second. A man must be fully committed to his wife, and the wife must be fully committed to her husband. You all should be best friends, prayer partners and recreational companions. Don't allow anyone, including your parents, to drive a wedge between the two of you. Thread your lives together. You must leave your mental, financial, emotional and spiritual dependence on your parents and transition that to your spouse. You and your spouse must be willing and able to stand, endure and cling to one another as if your lives depend on it.

Leaving and cleaving may be difficult for many, but you must do it because your marriage depends on it! Learn how to stand on your own. Men, it is your sole responsibility to provide for your household financially, emotionally and spiritually. You should never count on your parents to step in and fulfill your role. When challenges arise, cleave to your spouse like never before. When you neglect to disconnect from your parents or anyone that has the tendency to cause distractions, it can cause them to look down on your spouse. Assess every relationship in your life. Are there any relationships that drive a wedge between you and spouse? Are there any with which your spouse has concerns? If so, these are the ones that you must leave (forsake dependence upon, to release, leave behind and let go) behind for the sake of continually building a divorce proof marriage.

Applying Married Life – Leave & Cleave

In what ways do I need to forsake others and cleave to my wife?

_____
_____
_____
_____
_____

In what ways do I need to forsake others and cleave to my husband?

_____
_____
_____
_____
_____

Scriptures to Stand on to Always Cleave to One Another:

_____
_____

Our Confession to Forsake All Others and Cleave to One Another:

_____
_____
_____
_____
_____
_____
_____
_____
_____
_____

KEY 10: RESPECT YOUR SPOUSE

A key ingredient of love is respect. The Merriam-Webster Dictionary defines respect as *"a feeling or understanding that someone or something is important or serious, etc., and should be treated in an appropriate way; a high or special regard; the quality or state of being esteemed."* [7] When a husband shows love for his wife, it greatly increases her level of respect for him as commanded in Ephesians 5:33: *So again I say, each man must love his wife as he loves himself, and the wife must respect her husband.* When a wife shows respect for her husband, he is motivated to show immense love for her. A man needs the respect of his wife. He prospers and grows in godliness when she respects him. Wives, you win over your husband when you respect him verbally, emotionally, physically and spiritually. You must remember your role in the marriage. Allow him to lead you, and respect him even when you feel like he doesn't deserve it.

Ephesians 5:33 calls for the woman to respect her husband. But because the husband is called to love his wife as Christ loves the church, he, too, must respect his wife. Many times, you may not realize that your actions display blatant disrespect against your spouse. Mutual respect is a cornerstone of a successful marriage. It requires you to value the opinions of your spouse, consult with them before making decisions, and speak to them with honor. The loss of respect for your spouse has the power to negatively impact or even destroy your marriage. Love and respect go hand in hand. Here are some ways that you can disrespect your spouse without even knowing it.

---

[7] Source: http://www.merriam-webster.com/dictionary/respect

WAYS HUSBANDS DISRESPECT THEIR WIVES

1. **They neglect to properly provide for the family.**
2. **They do not allow their wives to help**. You must understand that her help is vital. Your wife has answers to some situations that you all are experiencing right now. You must allow her to help. She is a product of your intelligent choice. Don't be smart enough to marry her, but not smart enough to listen to her.
3. **They praise other women, but not their wives.**
4. **They expose their wives' weaknesses.** Protect your wife's area of limitations.
5. **They simply use their wives for sex.** Don't get yours off and leave her lying there unsatisfied. Men, it is not all about you when it comes to sexual pleasure. Know what your wife likes and do those things that please her. Play in the sand before diving right into the ocean. Foreplay is important.

WAYS WIVES DISRESPECT THEIR HUSBANDS

1. **They expect their husbands to know what they need.** Wives, your husbands cannot read your mind all of the time. Tell him what you need so that he can work to meet your needs.
2. **They express greater loyalty to outside authority figures** (i.e., pastor, bishop, boss, etc.). When you give more honor and respect to your pastor or boss, your husband feels like he is not important. He feels like you don't respect him.
3. **They resist their husbands' decisions and attempt to take a leadership role in the home.** It is your assignment to pray for your husband. Women are to be intercessors in the home. Even if you have a man that may have failed to take the lead, you are called to pray for your husband and keep him lifted up. If he falls, the Holy Spirit has it covered. You must rely on the Holy Spirit to catch you if you fall. If you don't let your husband lead, you tear him down.
4. **They correct their husbands in public or in the presence of other people.** If he is lying, tell him in private. Allow your

husband to exaggerate without lying. Never correct your husband in public.

5. **They resist physical affection.** Let him touch you when he desires. Your body belongs to your husband, and his body belongs to you.

Respect in marriage is essential to having godly order in your home. *For God is not a God of disorder but of peace...*(1 Corinthians 14:33). You respected your husband or wife when you first met and decided to marry. That level of respect should increase after marriage. Unfortunately, as time passes in marriages, spouses remove their restraints and cross the line way too often. At what point did your respect for one another diminish? How can you treat your spouse worse than you treat others? You grieve the Holy Spirit when you do such a thing! Don't become casual with your mate. Husbands are the heads and wives should respect them in their leading. Embrace humility, honor and respect to have a marriage that will last forever.

APPLYING MARRIED LIFE –
RESPECT YOUR SPOUSE

How can I better respect my wife?

_____
_____
_____
_____
_____

How can I better respect my husband?

_____
_____
_____
_____
_____

Scriptures to Stand on to Respect One Another:

_____
_____

Our Confession to Respect One Another:

_____
_____
_____
_____
_____
_____
_____
_____

PART THREE: THE JOURNEY

Enjoying the Journey

The thief comes only in order to steal, to kill and to destroy.
I came that they may have and enjoy life, and have it in
abundance, (to the full, till it overflows). (John 10:10 AMP)

Marital prosperity does not just happen. You must plan for success in marriage. You must be strategic about making your union one that is a match made in Heaven, experienced on earth. Kingdom marriages should be a divine illustration of God's purpose of becoming one flesh. When Christians get their marriages in order, they can counter-attack the enemy's schemes for marriage, including same-sex marriage. We have been marching against homosexual marriages, but failing secretly in our own Christian, heterosexual marriages. If we show the world God's design for marriage, Jesus will shine through our marriages. Many married couples are not enjoying marriage. They feel like they are imprisoned. What a horrible way to live! It's clear that you love your spouse; otherwise, you would not invest time in reading this book. It's more than a lack of love that breaks up marriages. It's that we have been missing the truth of God's Word, which has the power to fix every issue that arises in our marriages. God is the One who ordained and instituted marriage, so you cannot be successful at marriage apart from Him.

If you get a flat tire on the highway, you will not be able to fix it without the proper tools. It is the same in marriage. You must be equipped with the right tools. Your toolbox must include the Word of God, the truth of love, patience, grace, peace and longsuffering. You will also need the truth of, "I don't have to be right all the time." You also need to know when to speak and when to be quiet. You do not have to have everything in place before you enjoy your spouse. Marriage is the covenant in which you build your lives together. Even as you travel to the place where your goals, visions and dreams are accomplished, you can enjoy your journey if you align your marriage according to the principles of God's Word. If we apply these truths to our marriages, we can effectively display God's intended experience for marriage. We have declared war on divorce, and you must do the same! God hates marital separation and even through the greatest difficulties, you and your spouse must make covenant that divorce will never be an option. You may want to quit at times, but it is then that you must focus on the vows. It wasn't just a wedding, a cake, the champagne or the family. It's those vows that you spoke to your spouse in the presence of witnesses and God that you have to hold onto. *When you make a promise to God, don't delay in following through, for God takes no pleasure in fools. Keep all the promises you make to him. It is better to say nothing than to make a promise and not keep it* (Ecclesiastes 5:4-5). If you said, "I do," then you are obligated to keep your vows to God and to your spouse. When you honor God, He promises you an enjoyable and abundant life (Deuteronomy 5:33, John 10:10).

Zoe is life in its absolute sense. It is the life of God. If you are not living life according to God's Word, you will not experience the promised Zoe life in your marriage. Zoe life is the highest life, but that does not mean that it has to have the highest cost. Whatever your portion is in this season, you can enjoy life! Relational prosperity is learned. You must make the proper adjustments and concessions. You must yield and surrender, giving way to your spouse when necessary. Pride and selfishness will keep you waging war with your spouse when you should be yielding. *If the spirit of the ruler rise up against thee, leave not thy place; for yielding pacifieth great offences* (Ecclesiastes 10:4 KJV). It is not about who is right. Nor is it ever worth losing what you have because neither of you wants to compromise and yield to one another. Living in peace and harmony with your spouse is a learned skill. Marriage is a learning environment in which both partners grow and develop over time. Your careers and businesses are successful because over time, you have worked at it. Marriage requires the same attention, priority and tenacity. You have to train each other, and training takes time. It's funny how you can train others on the job and be patient with your employees for weeks *because you know* they are in training. Why won't you give this same grace to your spouse?

You never get a certificate of completion in marriage. Training never ends. Marriage gives you the gift of constant discovery of your spouse. You should always learn new things about your spouse and study the depths of their heart and soul. Don't stop on the surface! There are multiple layers to your spouse and until God comes back, you will never get through all of them. Where there is a lack of training, dysfunction is inevitable. Just as a job requires training to be successful in your role, the same applies in marriage. Training works two ways. The both of you must be willing to go through the unending course. Communication is the key to digging through each layer. It helps you understand the needs and desires of your spouse, and then equips you to meet those needs. The husband may want three meals a day; the wife may want her husband to provide a nice kitchen to cook. Anything that is weak is always bound to either give up or want to quit. You know when things are not working properly. If you sit and observe couples, you can tell if they are weak. It is evident in their conversations and how they deal with one another. When you refuse to submit to the training in your marriage, you break laws of courtesy and equity.

> *"You cry out, "Why doesn't the LORD accept my worship?" I'll tell you why! Because the LORD witnessed the vows you and your wife made when you were young. But you have been unfaithful to her, though she remained your faithful partner, the wife of your marriage vows. Didn't the LORD make you one with your wife? In body and spirit you are his. And what does he want? Godly children from your union. So guard your heart; remain loyal to the wife of your youth. "For I hate divorce!" says the LORD, the God of Israel. "To divorce your wife is to overwhelm her with cruelty," says the LORD of Heaven's Armies. "So guard your heart; do not be unfaithful to your wife." You have wearied the LORD with your words. "How have we wearied him?" you ask. You have wearied him by saying that all who do evil are good in the LORD's sight, and he is pleased with them. You*

have wearied him by asking, "Where is the God of justice?"
(Malachi 2:14-17)

The Lord sees how you treat your spouse. At some point, every spouse has dealt treacherously with their husband or wife. This is what hinders the God-ordained enjoyment in marriage. Sexual unfaithfulness is the lowest form of being treacherous with your spouse. You can break simple laws of courtesy and equity, which also takes you to the place of being unfaithful with your spouse. You violate laws of courtesy when you treat your coworkers, church family, friends or even strangers better than you treat your spouse. God's law requires that you honor your spouse just as you honor Christ. The two of you are one flesh. You cannot violate God's laws and expect to prosper. You break laws of equity when you strongly invest in other areas of your life, such as careers, ministry or other relationships, but refuse to put that same energy and investment into your marriage. This is a trick of the enemy. You send the message that your marriage is not important enough for you to make continual investments for it to be successful and enjoyable. Just as you would renovate or remodel your home to increase its value, you must also devote the same time and attention into making your marriage better. Don't ignore the required improvements for your marriage. You cannot continue to drive a car without getting it serviced regularly. It will break down! Consistent maintenance adds to the value and equity of the relationship. Most married couples don't have *real* relationships. Many aren't even friends! Don't let this be the makeup of your marriage. When you refuse to make the proper investments in your spouse, you allow someone else to come in and reap the benefits of your ventures.

Many couples tend to attack what is on the surface when they should take heed to what has hit their spirits. Once any type of offense hits your spirit, you will act treacherously against your husband or wife. Negativity in your spirit leads to infidelity, pornography, hiding money, lack of communication and more.

Guard your heart above all else, for it determines the course of your life.
(Proverbs 4:23)

Out of your heart flows the parameters, the issues and boundaries of life. Every positive or negative action for or against your spouse arises from what is deposited into your heart. Brothers, it is our responsibility to cover our wives. This isn't just limited to physical protection. She is delicate; she is the weaker vessel (1 Peter 3:7). Many couples don't enjoy marriage because whatever has hit the spirit of one or both spouses remains unresolved. Women are good with hiding what has hit their spirits. Most times, when you ask a woman if something is wrong, she denies it. You cannot heal a wound by ignoring it. You must deal in truth to fix your issues and move on to enjoying the journey of marriage. If all is not well, deal in truth and express your feelings. Wives, you must be honest with your husband.

THE ADJUSTMENTS – ENJOYING THE JOURNEY

Your marriage must be the priority in your life after God. Purposefully embrace and enjoy the good life with your spouse. This does not mean that you will not face obstacles in your life. But it does mean that you will continue to enjoy one another, despite the issues. Get an umbrella (the truth of the Word of God) and dance with one another in the rain!

Key adjustments that you and your spouse must make to enjoy the journey:

1. Understanding one another
2. Forgiving one another
3. Communicating with one another

ADJUSTMENT #1: UNDERSTANDING ONE ANOTHER

> *Getting wisdom is the wisest thing you can do! And whatever else you do, develop good judgment.* (Proverbs 4:7)

Many couples lack a thorough understanding of one other. This is the reason why spouses continue to have the same arguments and go in circles on the same road. When you become one, you must continually learn your spouse. What makes them tick? What inspires them the most? What makes them upset? How do you please them? What is their love language? Understanding the core of your spouse is an essential piece to enjoying your marriage. There are four areas of understanding. The first area is understanding one another as human beings.

> Then God said, "Let the earth produce every sort of animal, each producing offspring of the same kind—livestock, small animals that scurry along the ground, and wild animals." And that is what happened. (Genesis 1:24)

All humans are made in the image of God. We all share basic human needs. Hurt and bitterness manifest in marriage when one neglects to meet the needs of his or her spouse. Real hurt and rejection occurs when you respond to your spouse's expression for a need with selfishness and pride. Every human has a basic need for love. Everyone wants to be counted. Everyone wants to matter to someone else. We want to be regarded, feel valued, and feel chosen. We want to be seen and heard. We want people to seek after us and pursue us, just as God wants us to pursue Him. Everyone wants to be trusted and feel capable. If trust is lacking in a marriage, there is nothing to build upon. Everyone wants to be considered and consulted, respected and esteemed. They want security and stability. God wants all of these things, as well. We are all the same when it comes to human needs and we all have God components. You must understand the basic needs of your spouse. Men and women *want* these same things, but prefer them in a different manner.

The second area is understanding one another as male and female.

> So God created human beings in his own image. In the image of God he created them; male and female he created them. (Genesis 1:27)

Men and women are made differently. They choose differently, feel emotions differently and are uniquely wired. Men are more logical. They speak exactly what they think. Women are emotional feelers. They lead with their hearts and clearly express what they feel. Women say what is on their hearts, while men say what is on their minds. Men hear information. Women hear emotional experiences. If you don't understand that God made you and your spouse differently, you will endlessly war with one another.

A man's mind is like a filing cabinet. Give him a piece of information and he will pull it out when needed. A woman's mind is like a computer. She is not going to rest until the problem is resolved. She is going to ask you every day to complete the chore she requested until it is done. Men can be nomadic and change scenery overnight. Women need stability. They need to be settled because they become more attached to things than men do. Men also tend to be resentful. They will resent their wives before acknowledging their own responsibility. They will lash out in anger before they accept blame. Men will make their wives their targets and act against the guilt they refuse to bear. Because women are emotional creatures, they tend to be more prone to guilt. They tend to blame themselves and take responsibility for anything that goes wrong in the marriage, regardless of who is at fault. Men need to be told again and again, while women never forget. This can be dangerous for women because never forgetting can cause you to live in the past. What you don't forget, you will continue to bring back up in conversations with your husband.

The third area is understanding one another as individuals. Whether you are male or female, you are fearfully and wonderfully made. You are complex and unique. There is an inner delicacy that only you possess. The same is true of your spouse.

> You made all the delicate, inner parts of my body and knit me together in my mother's womb. Thank you for making me so wonderfully complex! Your workmanship is marvelous—how well I know it. You watched me as I was being formed in utter seclusion, as I was woven together in the dark of the womb. (Psalm 139:13-15)

Husbands and wives, you must comprehend that your spouse is unique. When you request them to conform to your preferences, you are molding your partner into someone other than who God created them to be. Don't attack the individual creation of your spouse. Appreciate who they are and what makes them unique. It will make your marriage sweeter and more enjoyable. There will be characteristics in your spouse that you love, and some others may be difficult for you to adjust to. But

God has given you the grace to love and appreciate everything that He has intricately placed in your life partner. What you are missing is probably in your spouse, and vice versa. Even in your differences, you both have attributes of God. You must appreciate the individual grace on your spouse's life in order for your marriage to succeed.

God knows what He is doing when He places two hearts, minds and bodies together to become one. He knows that there are different characteristics in each spouse that are required for success in your marriage. If one spouse is frugal and the other is excessive, you balance one another out. If both of you are excessive, you would probably be broke. Think carefully about whether you married a robot or a wonderfully-made creature with whom God paired you to walk through the journey of love and marriage.

Who you are today is a result of what you have experienced in every season of your life. From the moment that you were born, people wrote on the tablet of your heart. What your parents, friends, co-workers and others have said to you or about you played a major role in who you have become. If your mother or father was absent from your life, the effects of it have been written on the tablet of your heart. If you were emotionally or physically abused, it is on your heart. Everyone that you came in contact with wrote something on your heart. Maybe someone called you ugly in third grade, so you still spend an extra 30 minutes in the mirror so that you feel pretty.

When you get married, it is your responsibility to divulge every single thing that has been written on your heart. Your spouse has the right to know the experiences that have affected you, positively or negatively, so that he or she can become fully equipped to give you what you need to feel cherished, appreciated and loved. When you neglect to expose what is on your heart, those negative experiences come back to memory the moment your spouse does something that reminds you of your past. A lack of understanding one another as individuals has the tendency to cause couples to divorce, although they never stopped loving one another. Loving your spouse is not enough to be successful in marriage. Once you fully understand each other, you are better prepared to deal with one another.

You got married to serve one another and once you understand your spouse, you can better serve them according to their individual needs. Many people are good at hiding their past, acting as if their history has been magically erased. Your life partner should understand where you came from and whom they *really* married. God anointed you to deal with your spouse. On their worst day, they are graced to love you. You have to understand that through the good and bad, you made a determination in your heart that your marriage will work. That determination means everything! Promise each other that you all will get through *everything* you encounter *together*. Everything you need for your marriage to be successful will gravitate to you once you make that declaration to God and to one another. Things that you don't need will go away. Some of you are still connected to the wrong people. You have the wrong couples in your lives and you need to let some old friends go. Don't give the enemy any room to play in your marriage.

Adjustment #2: Forgiving One Another

Once you get to the place of understanding your spouse, you will be led to forgive and repent for things that you have done. Most couples were never trained how to have a successful, happy marriage rooted in Christ and love. Don't condemn yourself for finding it difficult to forgive. It is not easy, but every step you take toward walking in forgiveness demonstrates growth and maturity.

> *Even my best friend, the one I trusted completely, the one who shared my food, has turned against me.* (Psalm 41:9)

> *It is not an enemy who taunts me—I could bear that. It is not my foes who so arrogantly insult me—I could have hidden from them. Instead, it is you—my equal, my companion and close friend. What good fellowship we once enjoyed as we walked together to the house of God.* (Psalm 55:12-14)

All relationships have the potential to hurt, but those closest to you hurt you the most, especially when they violate and ignore basic human needs. Marriage is more than sharing a home and raising the children;

it is a friendship. When the hurt occurs, there is an immediate need for reconciliation. You cannot let the issue simmer because the root of bitterness will establish itself in your hearts and in your marriage. Time does not heal; it just gives the enemy more room to play in your marriage. You cannot heal a wound by saying it is not there.

> *They offer superficial treatments for my people's mortal wound. They give assurances of peace when there is no peace.* (Jeremiah 6:14)

The spouse that caused the hurt does not have the right to dictate how long it should take his or her spouse to get over it. The person that has been hurt doesn't have the right to dictate the degree of repentance. Forgiveness is not an emotion; it is a decision. The healing begins with the decision to forgive. The enemy will never make you feel like forgiving. The decision to forgive is sometimes made in the midst of offense. Forgiveness is a purposed, quality decision that you must make to excuse a fault. It is treating your spouse as if they are not guilty, even when they have gone too far or have caused incredible pain to your heart. Spouses, remember that forgiveness is a process that takes time. When a house catches on fire, the fire may be gone, but it still smells like smoke. That smoke is going to linger until you fix the damage. It takes time because there are layers to reparation. Many people think because they put the fire out, everything is okay, while the other spouse still smells like smoke. You have to deal with the residue of the pain and heartache that you inflicted upon your spouse.

> *Love prospers when a fault is forgiven, but dwelling on it separates close friends. (Proverbs 17:9)*
>
> *O Lord, you are so good, so ready to forgive, so full of unfailing love for all who ask for your help. (Psalm 86:5)*
>
> *Make allowance for each other's faults, and forgive anyone who offends you. Remember, the Lord forgave you, so you must forgive others. (Colossians 3:13)*

Instead, be kind to each other, tenderhearted, forgiving one another, just as God through Christ has forgiven you. (Ephesians 4:32)

So watch yourselves! If another believer sins, rebuke that person; then if there is repentance, forgive. Even if that person wrongs you seven times a day and each time turns again and asks forgiveness, you must forgive. (Luke 17:3-4)

Love is the opposite of not extending forgiveness to others. You must forgive because God has commanded you to do so. How can you forgive co-workers, friends or family, and not extend the same to your spouse? There are no limits to forgiveness, even if your spouse does not repent. Forgiveness is for *your* benefit. It frees you from bitterness and resentment. When your spouse acts outside of what God has ordained for marriage, they have chosen to be unaware and are thus, operating in ignorance. The Word of God demands you to forgive. Jesus Christ equipped you to forgive others, regardless of what they have done to you. Jesus did it and He expects the same from those that are the sons and daughters of Christ. God can fix *anything* in your marriage; it starts with forgiveness and then moves toward restoration. You know when you've grown in forgiveness because you no longer dwell on what your spouse did to you.

Enjoying the journey of marriage requires large doses of grace and patience. Many spouses forgive and expect immediate change, which probably will not happen. This is when you must extend the same grace and patience that Christ extends to you daily. Appreciate the small accomplishments and changes that you see in your partner. They probably won't go from A to Z instantaneously, but celebrate each milestone. It relieves you from anxiety and stress. While you are waiting for them to change, consult God about what He first wants to do in you. As the both of you grow together, your journey will become stronger, sweeter and more enjoyable.

ADJUSTMENT #3 – COMMUNICATING WITH ONE ANOTHER

You grow in your spiritual life by spending time with God, spending time in His Word and talking to Him daily. The same applies to your marriage. In the previous chapter on communication, I mentioned that it is impossible to have a healthy, prosperous relationship without effective communication. Couples must learn to communicate. Developing better communication in your marriage can be challenging. Take a moment to reflect on how and what you communicate with your spouse. Many couples spend time talking, but fail to fully understand one another. Dissect what you talk about. Do you talk about other people, jobs, church, or are you spending time talking about one another and your relationship? Spending more time discussing what matters most in your marriage better prepares you to enjoy the journey. When you know what matters to your spouse, and what will make your marriage successful, it becomes easier to meet the needs of one another. When you continually meet one another's needs, you make deposits in the love bank. But none of this can happen until you mature in your communication.

Communication means to transmit information, thoughts or feelings so that the information is satisfactorily received or understood. You must confirm that what you said is what the other understood. If this does not happen, spouses will operate off what they *thought* they heard rather than what was actually said. This opens the door to chaos and confusion. *Understand this, my dear brothers and sisters: You must all be quick to listen, slow to speak, and slow to get angry* (James 1:19). Don't always be so quick to respond. *Spouting off before listening to the facts is both shameful and foolish* (Proverbs 18:13). You can avoid a lot of misunderstanding, hurt and embarrassment if you learn to really listen to your spouse, process what they said, and then respond. Sometimes, saying nothing is best. You cannot misquote silence.

A gentle answer deflects anger, but harsh words make tempers flare. (Proverbs 15:1)

Don't use foul or abusive language. Let everything you say be good and helpful, so that your words will be an encouragement to those who hear them. (Ephesians 4:29)

A good person produces good things from the treasury of a good heart, and an evil person produces evil things from the treasury

of an evil heart. What you say flows from what is in your heart.
(Luke 6:45)

You brood of snakes! How could evil men like you speak what is good and right? For whatever is in your heart determines what you say. (Matthew 12:34)

The tongue can bring death or life; those who love to talk will reap the consequence. (Proverbs 18:21)

It is also crucial that you operate and communicate with an attitude of integrity. Men sometimes tend to omit information or only answer the questions that are asked. Women have a greater gift of discernment. When a woman asks you a question, it is likely that she already knows the answer. Don't put yourself further into the hole by lying and building wall after wall with lies. It will come back to bite you, so just tell the truth! Every lie has the potential to destroy. Be constructive and loving with your criticism.

Even in communication, you have to check your heart because out of the abundance of the heart, your mouth speaks. What you say to your spouse is what has penetrated your heart. You cannot blame your spouse. Your response is your responsibility. At the same time, whatever is in your heart is bound to come out. When hurt or frustration lies dormant in your heart, you must seek God for healing and deliverance. As the Holy Spirit gives you direction, work on your own heart. Allow Christ to heal you in any areas where you need to grow. Therefore, when you are tested, the characteristics of Christ will come out. This will prevent folly, foolishness and corrupt communication in your marriage. You always have a part to play in how you communicate with your spouse. When you are reckless with your speaking, you are murdering your spouse. (Proverbs 18:21) You will eat the fruit of what you say, so choose your words carefully. Words do hurt!

God richly provides you with everything for your enjoyment (1Timothy 6:17 NIV). That includes your marriage. God has equipped you with everything you need to make your marriage successful. The same God that provided Abraham, Sarah, Hannah, Isaac and Jacob with all that they stood in faith for will also provide for you. You must stand in faith that your marriage will thrive, not just survive. God is a Father of love and because marriage was created to exhibit a mirrored image of His love for us, He wants you to enjoy every moment of it. He wants you both happy, whole, healthy and prosperous. He wants you to have fun. He wants you to experience abundance–not just in physical things–but an abundance of love, peace, communication, understanding, wisdom and pleasure in your marriage.

Marriage is a continual work! It is similar to our relationship with Christ. When you get saved, you don't continue to do the same things that you did when you were in the world. Your goal should be to grow closer to Christ and to become more like Him. In order to become like Christ, you must fully know His characteristics, what disappoints Him, what pleases Him and most importantly, you must fully experience God working in your life. Over time, you develop a very intimate relationship with Him. You develop that relationship by spending time in His Word and in prayer. It is the same with your spouse. After you both have said, "I do," the work begins. You learn the intimate details of one another's heart and mind by talking to one another, asking the right questions, serving one another and doing whatever you must to please each other. After God, nothing comes before your spouse, including your children. You have committed to love, honor and respect one another. Now, if you have not already done so, commit to enjoying the journey with your spouse. God brought you two together for a purpose. You must walk out every plan that God intended for you all as a union and a family. You cannot fulfill God's vision for the union separately.

A fun, loving marriage is built on the decisions you make. The decision to enjoy the journey comes from the same resolve that divorce is not an option. Stop focusing on changing one another or waiting until the conditions are perfect before you decide to enjoy your marriage. *Farmers who wait for perfect weather never plant. If they watch every cloud, they never harvest* (Ecclesiastes 11:4). Simply agree to enjoy life and each other. Make the decision to avoid ruts and routine in marriage.

Life comes with great responsibility, but don't allow responsibility to trump the passion and fun in your marriage. Break routine with spontaneous and creative date nights. Make new experiences that allow you and your spouse to dream and play together. You must also make the decision to value the needs and desires of one another. Marriage was created to be a lifetime of sharing love, experiences and memories. Husbands, whatever you did to get your wife, you must continue doing, but at a higher level. Wives, you must continue to do what you did to initially garner the attention of your husband. If you both remember that you got married to serve one another, let go of your selfish ways and commit to your decisions, your marriage will be enjoyable, even through the challenges. It is sad to be married and not enjoy the companionship that God has given to you.

> *Live happily with the woman you love through all the meaningless days of life that God has given you under the sun. The wife God gives you is your reward for all your earthly toil.* (Ecclesiastes 9:9)

CONCLUSION

Congratulations! I pray that you have enjoyed this book and that it has strengthened your marriage. If you are not married, I pray it has prepared you to have a successful marriage in the future. You are equipped with everything you need to do the work and have a fruitful, fun marriage. Take what you've learned and apply it, bit by bit. Restoration does not come overnight. It takes time and investment. Marriage takes work, but it is truly worth the sacrifice. You both have to commit to one another that you are going to do the work in your marriage. You have to be willing to die to your needs and desires to meet the needs of your spouse. I want to hear great testimonies of what God has done in your marriage. A great seed has been planted in your marriage, and the enemy is mad. But, you shall see a harvest.

Get accountability partners in your marriage. Find a godly couple that will speak into your relationship, pray for you both and hold you accountable to be the partners that God has destined you to be. Do not overlook the progress, the progressive power of the Word of God. Something has been deposited into your heart by reading this book. The Word, once received, will begin to grow. Encourage one another when you see progress.

London and I are overjoyed that you have completed this book! We are certain that your marriage is growing and is stronger than ever before. This is only the beginning of your journey, and we are certain that divorce will never be your portion. We want to take this opportunity to personally extend an invite to attend any of our Married Life Chicago events. If you are not in the area, many of our events have live broadcasting. It is a blessing to know that you and your spouse have joined us in declaring war on divorce. May God bless, ignite, restore and revitalize your marriage and may it be everlasting!

ABOUT MARRIED LIFE CHICAGO

Married Life is a Christian-based initiative that provides practical knowledge on preserving the sacred covenant of marriage. It is open to the public at large and unmarried individuals who wish to be married soon are encouraged to participate as well.

Married Life has declared war on divorce. The mission of Married Life is to increase the number of happily married couples, decrease the percentage of divorces in society, and further equip men and women with wisdom to meet each other's needs in a fruitful and successful marriage.

Married Life is a community outreach program funded by Lifeline Church, located in Cicero, IL, a western suburb of Chicago. A team of married couples under the leadership of Reggie and London Royal organizes it.

CPSIA information can be obtained
at www.ICGtesting.com
Printed in the USA
FSOW01n0640120817
37474FS